Testimonials for *Life's One Law*

"With the help of Dr. Agrios and his framework, I was able to understand my sabotaging trait that was preventing me from achieving my desired results, no matter how much energy I put into it ... I was able to clear my mental blocks, increase my energy levels and achieve an immediate 25% growth in my business in a span of 3 months."
—Radhakrishnan KG, Founder, WebNamaste Consulting Pvt Ltd.

"This program presented me with an "AHA" moment. In personal and business situations, learning to uncover my antidote for resolving conflicts produced immediate and optimal results ... I have truly been transformed ..."
—Janice Volk, Physical Therapist

"I increased my income by 76.32% within the first month using Dr. Agrios' Six Step Blueprint to solve any problem. With it, I was able to understand where I was sabotaging myself and how to switch it off instantly. It is truly amazing!"
—Thomas Madden, Esq., Divorce Attorney

"A business heals as a person makes their own personal enhancements. Dr. Agrios' unique approach and process helped me see where I was allowing stress to deplete my energy and gave me the tools to correct the imbalance."
—Jason Hoffman, Managing Partner and Chief Instructor, The Max Challenge

"Using Dr. Agrios' method to find my Antidote had an immediate impact on me. Right away I noticed a change in how I handled stress at work and in my personal life ... the Antidote helped me develop a clearer strategy for furthering my career."
—Thomas Whalen, VP, Commercial Real Estate Bond Trading

"Dr. Agrios taught me how to identify what my triggers are so I can be aware of them and taught me what my Antidote is, so I can deal with the stresses in my life in a much-more productive way … two years later, my life is much more put together because I use my Antidote on a regular basis. I no longer feel out of control …"
—C.J. Arditi, Legal Shield National, Field Trainer

"Being a single mother with two small children has different challenges than my business. I was amazed how the Antidote, which helped my business, also caused my personal life to be calmer and much more manageable. Things have never been better … I use the Antidote because it always works!"
—Rachel Cluna, CEO/Owner RAC Consulting

"The Antidote gave me ways to make some crucial decisions in my life and in my practice which worked every time … Then I discovered my solution … instead of brushing it off as 'too simple,' I put it into action and there I saw the genius of Dr Agrios' work. Simple is powerful!"
—Aristotelis E. Vlahos, M.D., Board Certified Cardiologist

"Once I started to use my Antidote, it quickly started to work. I couldn't believe not only how simple it was to use but the powerful results I was achieving. Yes! It can be that simple!"
—Kosta Linardakis, DC, Chiropractor

"Dr. Agrios' program enabled me to identify what was holding me back in life, so that I could direct my time and talent accordingly. The Antidote was the main reason I found that part of me. I highly recommend this program."
—Harry Chambarry, Actor

LIFE'S ONE LAW

Nature's Blueprint for Repeatable Success in Life and Business

Dr. Philip Agrios

ISBN 978-1-7322392-0-3

Published by Health Switch Publishing, Jackson, New Jersey.

Cover design and interior images by Jo Lis, Interactive and Branding Expert, www.josephlis.com.

Additional interior images by Barbara A. Cucinelli, All American Print and Copy Center, LLC, New Jersey

Editing and formatting by The Write Room, LLC, New Jersey, www.thewriteroom.com

Excerpt from *A Return To Love* used by permission from Marianne Williamson.

Disclaimer

The information given and discussed in this book is not intended to be, nor should it in any way be construed to be a cure, antidote, remedy, answer or otherwise be considered to be a substitute for professional therapy, treatment and/or counseling. The achievement statements and examples in this book are not intended to represent or guarantee that everyone will achieve the same results. Each individual's success will be determined by his or her desire, dedication, effort and motivation to work and follow recommendations. There is no guarantee you will duplicate the results stated here.

For Educational purposes only. Not intended to treat, diagnose, cure or prevent any disease. Its intent is to give general information regarding a discovery made by Dr. Philip Agrios and to disseminate such information to the general public. No claims or representations are made by Dr. Philip Agrios regarding product performance or benefits.

The names of the individuals in this book have been changed.

DEDICATION

My life would have been even more of a struggle if I did not have certain people in it to help me through some of those tough times. I want to thank all of you.

To my two beautiful and loving daughters, Chelsea and Alexia, you are my life. Without you, life would not be fulfilling. I love you!

To my stepdaughter, Natalie, many thanks for your contributions and editorial guidance throughout the process of writing this book.

To my loving fiancée, PJ, whose support and unconditional love has allowed me to start on my new journey to bring Life's One Law to the masses. You make my life complete. I love you!

Nature does not hurry, yet everything is accomplished.

–Lao Tsu

CONTENTS

ABOUT THE AUTHOR xi

FOREWORD xiii

INTRODUCTION xviii

SECTION 1:
PERCEPTION

How Uncomfortable Is Your Perception? 3

Do You Really Believe That? 9

Are You Willing To Pay This Price For Success? 15

SECTION 2:
INTRODUCING NATURE'S BLUEPRINT

How Nature's Blueprint Was Discovered 25

Understanding Nature's Blueprint 28

Our Blueprint For Repeatable Success 34

Why Failure Is Essential For Your Insight 42

SECTION 3:
UTILIZING NATURE'S BLUEPRINT

Summer: Time To Decide 53

Harvest : Time To Pay Yourself 59

Autumn: Time To Detach From What's Not Working 65

Winter: Be Still And Notice The Power 83

Relinquis: Time To Show Them What You Got 91

Spring: Create A Rapport 99

Summer: Are You Happy With Your End Result? 106

The Seasons Driven By Fear 112

Summary Of The True And Fear Seasons 128

SECTION 4:
LIFE'S ONE LAW

Sell Confidently & Succeed Repeatably 134
Can Life Be This Simple? 152
The Sabotaging Trait And Its Antidote 160
The Six Seasons Are The Three Principles 173
Your Company Has A Sabotaging Trait 181
What Would You Do With A Rotten Tomato? 187

SECTION 5:
APPLY THE TEACHINGS OF THIS BOOK

Now Apply It 199
Tapping Into Abundance 204

SECTION 6:
EXPLANATION OF TERMS

Quick Reference Of Life's One Law 215
Additional Recommendations 220

INDEX

ABOUT THE AUTHOR

Philip C. Agrios, DC, DACBSP is a Personal & Business Advisor, author and speaker and teaches his clients how to stop sabotaging themselves and get out of their own way so they can have more freedom. His discovery of The 6 Step Problem-Solving Blueprint allows him to quickly and precising pinpoint the blocks that surround people in their business and personal life.

Dr. Agrios' life experiences, although filled with many tragic events, have prompted him to dedicate his life to teaching his discovery. He has created seminars, internet courses and other avenues so others may be helped using the same principles as he did to continue on their journey of life, thereby attaining optimal health, wealth and happiness.

He shares his perspective not only from a clinical point of view but provides his clients with pertinent examples taken from his own life experiences.

A graduate of Logan College of Chiropractic, Chesterfield, Missouri, Dr. Agrios earned his Doctor of Chiropractic (DC) degree in 1985. Prior to his studies at Logan, he attended the University of Scranton, Scranton, Pennsylvania.

In 2000, Dr. Agrios was no longer able to practice chiropractic due to a disability. He sold his practice to his competitors and attained the position of Marketing Director. Marketing proved not to be rewarding and he felt he was not fulfilling his life's purpose. At that point, he believed he was destined to begin the quest to reverse his own disability.

Throughout the following year, he embarked upon his program encompassing a regime of nutritional therapy, chiropractic treatment and a specialized strengthening program. However, he knew that to be completely cured, he needed to treat not only his physical body, but the mental and spiritual aspects of himself as well.

He did the latter through applying what he calls, "*Life's One Law*," his discovery from a decade prior. This unique combination enabled him to resume his practice and continue to help others through his education, training and personal experience.

Dr. Agrios did return to practicing chiropractic a few years later and as fate had it, started to attract more chronically ill patients with conditions similar to his own. It took another decade or so to refine his treatment by using the same methods of curing his own conditions and applying them to his patients.

He realized that the personal mentoring component of his treatment was the main reason for the high success rates. Furthermore, as patients were having successful outcomes in their health and personal lives, he recognized that those who were business owners, executives and sales professionals were having breakthroughs in the career aspects of their lives.

He decided to focus his complete attention on the principles of *Life's One Law* and teach them to the masses. He knew he would have more of an impact proving his hypothesis and creating the awareness of how life is not as complicated as it seems. As a result, he was inspired to create different avenues to teach others how to overcome severe obstacles as he did.

FOREWORD

Life's One Law is filled with Dr. Philip Agrios' own innovative principles, techniques, and strategies for transformational growth in business and relationships. This groundbreaking material is to be reflected on by readers and is destined to inspire much fruit for all who choose to embrace the exercises and insights Dr. Agrios has to offer.

Sharing the gift of *Life's One Law* is Dr. Agrios' gift to the world. It is his purpose. For over a decade, Dr. Agrios has refined his original idea with much depth to facilitate genuine transformation in his readers.

The actual "Law" is a discovery by Dr. Agrios that allows individuals to take back control of their lives, particularly in response to stress. In this book, he skillfully walks the reader through identifying what he defines as their personal self-sabotaging trait, and with that information, the reader learns why things do not seem to be working out well in their life.

With precision, Dr. Agrios then walks the reader through identifying their stress antidote which is the exact opposite of the self-sabotaging trait.

The role of nature and its seasons plays a key part in this process and is skillfully and creatively woven into Dr. Agrios' blueprint for success. Dr. Agrios defines six seasons and out of these seasons, three basic governing principles are created which encompass *Life's One Law*.

Dr. Agrios uses the six seasons to guide the reader with specific goals to be completed for both business and personal growth. He teaches us how to use each season in an inspiring way. For a business, Summer is production season. Harvest follows, a time to gather as well as replenish. You will also learn about "Relinquis", or the season of "burning desire," as you release the power within while forgiving yourself and extending gratitude.

Dr. Agrios helps readers alter their thinking and they become unknowingly compelled to express gratitude for the actual desire to change. This cognitive shift in fact changes energy, which transforms what and how we attract.

Dr. Agrios also identifies a personality stress sequence for a business as he illustrates how his personal sabotaging trait and his business' sabotaging trait were in conflict, actually feeding off each other. He illustrates resolution in an encouraging way.

Identifying sabotaging traits and finding the antidote is a hidden secret of *Life's One Law*. I can attest from direct experience, when I became aware of my sabotaging trait, I experienced relief- and lasting change, both personally and professionally. I became aware of my subconscious tendency to put everyone else before me. I realized the difference between caring deeply for others and sabotaging myself. I recognized that decisions I had made in the past were heavily influenced by my trigger trait, and with the help of Dr. Agrios blueprint I found awareness- and relief- almost instantaneously. Now, years later, I am able to maintain healthy boundaries and am so much more empowered and effective in life, freed up from my past tendency to self-sabotage.

Dr. Agrios has special wisdom and insights for overcoming trials and tribulations. He sees those obstacles as gifts, embracing the challenges offered as foundational for serious growth, mastery and healing.

On a deeper level, this book is a hero's journey. In the face of unspeakable pain and loss, Dr. Agrios reached deep within, made a conscious decision to never quit, and developed the timeless principle of *Life's One Law*. He used and continues to use these principles to transform his own life. His purpose now is to now share these principles with all destined to receive his gift.

Dr. Mary Zennett

Author, *Health For US All: The Transformation of US Health Care*

Founder, Global Health, LLC

INTRODUCTION

I want to first thank you for reading my book. It is born from my experiences; I did not write this book from textbook learning only; I lived it. I have experienced many stressful events ... simultaneously. They did not all happen at once, but they existed in different degrees within the same time frame.

I felt that no matter what I did, who I talked to, or how much I prayed, nothing seemed to help me get through those difficult times. I had many conversations with my Higher Power, including screaming in prayer and asking, "What is happening? How can I get through this?" I even fell into a depression without even knowing it until a psychologist mentioned it to me.

I felt lost and helpless. I was surviving on a daily basis. That is, until the day I realized I had to change something major in my life. I still do not know for certain how it happened. Perhaps the shock and reality of my dad dying of brain cancer forced me to realize that my own survival depended upon changing my problems into learning experiences. I learned through his suffering that if my dad, a young 71-year-old who walked four miles a day and was very giving to others, could suddenly experience such a severe, life-threatening circumstance, then life, no matter how good or bad it was, could always be worse. To me, this was a frightening reflection, one of the most jolting thoughts I had ever experienced.

I thought long and hard, while sitting at his bedside, about what was going to happen to me as I faced worry, anxiety and self-pity. I could no longer practice chiropractic medicine because of a physical disability. Three physicians told me I would never practice again.

I remember the day I came to this realization. It was cold and brisk, and the wind hit my back as I locked the door of my clinic for the very last time. I stepped back and looked up at the bold white letters displaying the words, "Agrios Chiropractic and Rehabilitation Center." As I stared numbly at these words, I thought back to the day that I turned that same lock to the open position.

My clinic started with one suite and quickly grew to encompass the entire left side of the building, becoming a 2700-square-foot clinic that housed medical doctors, physical therapists, nutritionists and other health professionals; it was a thriving practice that helped many patients.

As I shook my head in disbelief, a bittersweet smile on my face, I contemplated the ambitious dreams and grand aspirations I envisioned when I first opened the doors as a practicing chiropractic physician. But there I was, closing the doors on my practice for good, due to a disability that I had developed. "How did this happen? This practice was my baby," I said under my breath.

It felt like one of my kids died, and I would never have the opportunity to treat patients again. I had never experienced this type of hopelessness before.

I turned around and walked through the parking lot to my car. It felt like I had lost the biggest game of my life. Fifteen years of practicing plus years of study down the tubes and I had no idea what my next move would be. Never in my wildest dreams would I have suspected that the Universe had a different path planned for me.

The years prior to this had taken a toll on me. A volatile marriage. The brain tumor that claimed my father. I was my ailing mother's primary caregiver for seven years and watched her suffer and eventually die from COPD. Finally, a three-year legal battle that dismantled my multi-discipline practice, plus financial difficulty and other challenges caused so much stress that I finally broke -- mentally, physically and spiritually.

At that breaking point, I was diagnosed with thoracic outlet syndrome on both sides of my body which caused weakness and numbness down both my extremities as well as carpel tunnel syndrome in both hands, leaving me with severe pain and limited use of my hands. Since conventional therapy had failed, I was told my only option was surgery, which did not have a high success rate.

Inflammation ran rampant causing fatigue and pains throughout my body. When I got out of bed, my feet hurt so much I thought I was walking on broken glass. On top of that, I was told I was clinically depressed. It all left me wondering what kind of game the Universe was playing on me. I was only in my late 30's.

As the months went by, I realized that there had to be some type of gift that I was given from all this; to have so much chaos and to lose so much, there must be a purpose. I knew this had to be so, because of reading and watching the biographies of other successful people. Many of them took devastating situations and used them to not only better themselves but others.

I also took note of biographies of infamous people who had similar choices to make, but took a different path -- the path of destruction. Is that where I wanted to go? Absolutely not!

I was at that same pivotal point in the crossroad, and I began searching for answers by meditating, listening to motivational speakers, and praying. However, it helped for only a little while. This intense and addicting roller coaster of emotions would again consume me, causing me to flip flop between inspiration and desperation.

To keep my sanity, I started to write about suffering. I immersed myself into elaborating on my previous discovery regarding human behavior. It was only by doing this I finally realized the gift within losing my practice; it was for me to have time to dive deeper into my work.

In that work, I discovered a law which not only the entire universe follows, but human behavior as well. All my years of personal suffering allowed me to develop and clearly understand its simple but powerful potential to help millions of people.

The more I dove into this concept, the more I began to realize why and how my past decisions led me to my then present-day circumstances. Without them, I would have never discovered nor had the time to fully develop my hypothesis.

By applying this discovery to my own situation, along with chiropractic care, specialized nutritional therapy and a specific exercise program, I was able to start practicing again. However, this time, I was not the same doctor, nor the same person.

Things started to improve and I felt I was moving down the right path. Finally, my dreams seemed that they may come to fruition.

Then, as quickly as positive change started to come, it left. I found myself dealing with more challenges, wondering if I would ever really understand how life really worked. I was now faced with the passing of my mom, personal difficulties with my children, a divorce, and problems with my place of employment creating more financial strain. I remember sitting on my couch feeling that hopelessness I experienced the day I turned the lock on my clinic's door for the last time.

However, something was different. This time, I knew there was a light at the end of the tunnel. It was screaming so loud I couldn't understand what it was saying. Finally, it became clear: my work was not complete!

There was more to be discovered. Throwing myself into my discovery, trying to find out what I was missing, more information came to me and allowed me to see more clearly and learn exactly what I had to do.

During that time, I met my fiancée, left my employment situation and opened up my own practice again. This time though, instead of primarily practicing chiropractic and only periodically teaching my discovery to patients, I incorporated it into my practice. Gradually, I began to specialize in treating chronically ill patients while decreasing the treatment of acute based conditions.

I soon fully immersed myself in this field and gave my discovery a name, *Life's One Law*. I knew at that time that my ultimate purpose was to start guiding chronically ill patients to find the same clarity and gift within their own illnesses and life's challenges as I did.

As I began treating patient after patient with very high success rates, over time, it became clear how my path that began on that brisk cold February day, led me to my true destiny which had finally been revealed to me.

I now knew wholeheartedly that I was meant to bring *Life's One Law* to the masses.

Then as my patients who were business owners, executives and sales professionals were receiving improvement in their personal life, they were also making breakthroughs in their businesses. It was then I decided to leave the healthcare field and be a Personal & Business Advisor.

We live in a dichotomous world – up/down, left/right, in/out, yin/ yang. You have the choice of looking at the side that you determine is good or bad, a benefit or a detriment.

You have the full choice to determine if your right is better than your left or is going up better than going down. If you really think about it, each side has no meaning until you place a meaning on it at that moment in time.

Everything is neutral until you stamp the label of "Good" or "Bad" on it, as it is all based on your knowledge and understanding of your past experiences at that moment. This is why something that you thought that was awful can be thought of being awesome because your knowledge and understanding changed regarding it.

If you don't evolve, you dissolve. Each side is as important as the other, depending on what is needed for your experience. Each happens at the exact same time, but in different aspects of your life. Whatever you focus on and whatever meaning you give it, is now forever expressed as your daily reality.

Just as my reality back then was a dissolution of old perceptions and meanings which I interpreted as horrific; at the same time, I was conversely evolving or developing new perceptions that illuminated the path that the Universe had laid before me.

I thought I had to choose whether or not I was evolving or dissolving instead of what I truly needed to do. It was trusting the Universe and allowing my new destiny to unfold so that I could guide others through their own evolution and dissolution in a clearer and simpler way. If not for all that had happened, all of what I am doing now would have not manifested.

I realized during those times how much worse things were about to become if I did not change my own thought process. I knew I could not go through these many circumstances and for a lengthy period of time without some good or bad coming out of it. I knew deep down that it was my choice to determine if these situations were "good" or "bad." I knew with absolute certainty that I had to decide how I would view those choices. The choices belonged to me and no one else.

I knew that from these extreme, life-altering occurrences, I could help others who were faced with similar situations.

As a chiropractor, I had technical knowledge of the body from many years of formal study, particularly how the mind affects the body. Then, with my training in functional medicine and working with chronically ill patients, knowing that although I was once disabled, I was once again living a normal life without pain, I fine-tuned my discovery.

I had these personal experiences waiting to be defined, to be given proper meaning and definition. Despite all of the chaos and confusion I was living through, I knew there had to be my purpose somewhere waiting to be discovered.

I finally found my purpose, my life's ability to evolve as a human being and to help others evolve with me if they chose to do so.

So, I made a decision. I decided to always find the benefit in the situations that were occurring in my life. My life has turned around. I am fully grateful for all of those who came into my life whether good or bad, who allowed me to reclaim my life.

Now, it's time for you to also make a decision. Are you going to allow the fear of change to rule your life, rewarding you with your disease, heartache or depression, or are you going to pay the price to claim your due reward – purpose, peace and service? It is that straightforward.

I wrote this book to give you an insight of how *Life's One Law*—Nature's Blueprint for Repeatable Success, can help you to reclaim those treasures.

Dr. Philip Agrios

April 2018

SECTION 1: PERCEPTION

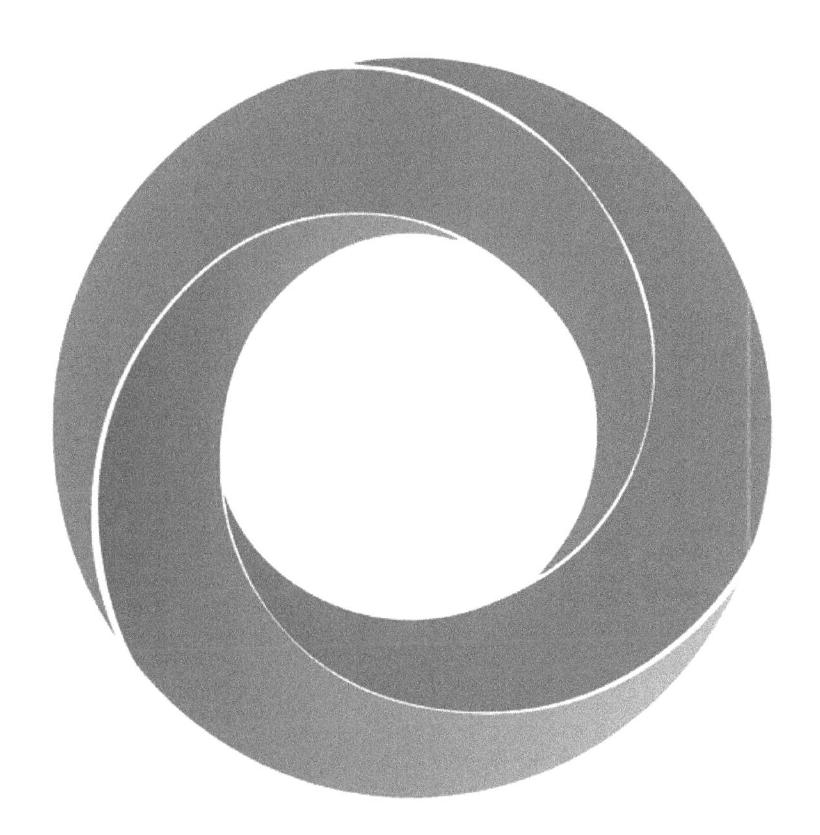

CHAPTER ONE

HOW UNCOMFORTABLE IS YOUR PERCEPTION?

It's 3:03 AM. The piercing red numbers of my alarm clock won't let me forget. Except for that red reflecting on the fan above my bed, it's dark. Even the moon won't come out on this terrifying night.

The familiar scenario keeps playing out in my head: I catastrophize my business' future, hoping that some mystical being will come out and save me from the humiliation of debtors and repossession.

It seems that no matter my past behavior the same results continue to arise, and I can't seem to learn from my mistakes. I can't get out of the hamster wheel of being or feeling behind.

I bury my head in the covers and pretend everything will be okay. Or not!

Why do we end up in the same place no matter how many training sessions we attend, business consultants we listen to, or psychics we consult? It seems like we are comfortable here despite dreaming of bigger and better things. We *want* happiness, but can't seem to *obtain it.*

In my consults with patients, the mere suggestion that they were comfortable in their own misery turned their eyes as red as that alarm clock.

To suggest that they were *comfortable* being *uncomfortable* and vice versa seemed ludicrous. "All I want is a better life for my family and me," they'd say to me. "How could you even suggest it's my fault?" Their perception was that things always happened *to them* and nothing ever was coming *from them.*

We *want* happiness, but can't seem to obtain it.

Here's my question: if you have no control over something, can you change it? No. But, you can control your *perception* of an issue and from there, start to change your outcomes.

My patient Beverly had a medical practice. Needless to say, it was not doing very well. Her practice was not as busy as she wanted. She was married with a nine-year-old daughter, plus she had an autoimmune disease which I was helping her treat with nutrition. As with every patient, she had to go through my personal mentoring program.

Eventually her health improved, and she was feeling better, but the success of her practice didn't budge. After a conversation, she came to realize that the issue came down to a struggle between spending time with her daughter and spending more time working.

As it is for so many mothers, juggling quality time between the family and work causes undue stress to which there seems to be no answer.

But once I suggested she sit down with her daughter and create a written contract outlining the hours she would spend with her and the numbers of hours she would spend on her practice, something magical started to happen.

Within a couple of weeks, her practice started to grow. And within less than a year she had to move to another building because it was too small.

So, what was the barrier that stopped her growth? No, not her daughter.

It was her *perception*. She perceived that if her business grew she would be a bad mom because she would spend less time with her daughter, a belief that resonated from her mother and grandmother. In a way, Beverly got permission from her daughter to be successful by accepting that her mom had a business and it was not going to compete with her time. It was like a sibling rivalry. Once Beverly allowed herself to see the success of business and the success of motherhood through her daughter's eyes, she was able to let go of the guilt and flourish in all aspects of her life.

Beverly perceived being successful as more uncomfortable than the balancing act. She was comfortable being uncomfortable and felt she had no control over the situation.

But she did.

And so do you.

This book will show you a discovery I made decades ago. By working with thousands of patients, I was able to harness the secret of nature. This is not a cliché but what I call the actual blueprint that nature uses to be successful year after year.

I will show you how to follow step-by-step this same blueprint that has created our successes and our failures. Imagine knowing why you failed and how to avoid those steps and why you succeeded and how to duplicate it.

The forests do not need our help and have mechanisms already built in to survive the harshest storms and take advantage of the most beautiful days. For millions of years they have done this, all because of a specific blueprint they use that has stood the test of time.

If you had this blueprint for your business, your career, your life, and the lives of your loved ones, what would you do with it? What would you be able to accomplish? Would you welcome it, be wary of it, or reject it?

This blueprint will teach you how to embrace your sufferings and turn them into benefits. It will give you a simple answer to what to do next in any situation regarding your work, business, or your personal life.

Note that when I use the word, "business" in this book, you can substitute it with "career" or "job." This information is valuable to anyone.

Think about situations you encounter with your boss, co-workers, or even relatives and how putting the blueprint into practice can affect them. Using the examples I've provided and then seeing how they pertain to your own business and personal circumstances will help you get the most out of this book.

By understanding the inner workings of your Self and how they relate to your business and personal life, you can take control and know exactly what to do to change your outcome. You'll discover why you react the way you do and why you have made the decisions in the past that led to favorable and unfavorable consequences.

Why do you continually sabotage your success and get in your own way? Just what is producing this protective cascade of spontaneous thoughts, feelings and actions within you? How do negative, detrimental behaviors develop? I will show you exactly how you push the first behavioral domino, your Sabotaging Trait which sets off a chain-reaction stress response that leads to negative behaviors.

I will teach you about your individualized Antidote to your Sabotaging Trait so that you will stop missing opportunities again and again. Learn how this one domino sets off a chain reaction of increased profitability in your business and personal life.

I will show you how I uncovered this blueprint by discovering there are really six seasons of nature, not the four we know. This revelation then led me to understand that the seasons were created by three basic principles that make up the universe. It showed me how life really works. These three principles then work together simultaneously creating – as the title of the book reveals – *Life's One Law*. I will elaborate on this law in greater detail later in the book.

There is no way of avoiding them. Every moment you are in a season. It can last for one second or for years. The transition from season to season does not necessarily follow the time that nature follows because you have in some cases the ability to increase or decrease the duration. Once you know how to utilize it to the fullest, you will then know what to do next because the other season is waiting to be part of your life.

These seasons affect everything from the atoms to the galaxies. They affect and guide us through our behaviors and once you understand this fully, you can take control of your behavior — which can give you the control of your outcomes.

How do I know this? I live it myself and have shared it with my patients for decades.

The path of this discovery has not been an easy one. With every triumph I would make, a devastating failure would ensue to show me something so powerful and simplistic that I felt compelled to continue the search. Many times, I would have no idea what I was looking for but nonetheless I was driven to find it.

The decisions I made not only affected my life but the lives of every individual who entered it, some for good and others not so good. The suffering I endured affected them – and through this suffering some relationships were made and cemented while others were blown apart.

Often, I wanted to quit, and I did, but for only brief moments. It felt like I was on a conveyor belt that would not allow me to exit. It was the cycles of these six seasons that were driving me.

Every time I would resist, it would cause strife in my life. When I just allowed, it would take me to the place I needed to be. Even though I thought there was a faster and shorter way, I realized in hindsight that I needed to take that path to pick up the needed experience to find the next treasure trove of information.

The more I uncovered, the more I would ask my family, friends and patients if they too were going through these same experiences. When I found what worked for me, I would ask if I could try it on them. This was the start of my research to determine whether what I was uncovering was a coincidence or a something more. To my astonishment, there was a pattern that everything and everyone was following. That would mean if I had the pattern, then I could guide others to understanding the meaning in their life and how to change it. This is what I have discovered and would like to take you on a journey through this book and show you just that.

However, first we must start with the discussion of perception. This is where we not only form our barriers of thought but disassemble them to create a new direction we desire to achieve.

How have your perceptions shaped your business and your life up to this point? Would you like to have control over them or are you comfortable being controlled?

CHAPTER TWO

DO YOU REALLY BELIEVE THAT?

When we consider our daily thought processes and the countless commands or decisions taking place, there is a powerful tool in charge of our decisions. That tool is:

PERCEPTION!

"Perception" is the basis of all our reasoning, our commands, and our decisions. Perception is responsible for how we act or react.

The accumulation of our knowledge and understanding from past experiences come together to create our current reality. And our reality determines our impression of whether or not a situation is dangerous or beneficial.

Have you ever seen someone in the distance and thought to yourself, *I don't know what it is about that guy, but I don't like him.* What reason do you have to think that? You haven't even met him.

Well, he may remind you of someone. He may have the demeanor or physical traits of an old boyfriend, ex-spouse, in-law, or a previous boss.

The reality that this person is a threat has been created in your mind by your perception. Whether it's ultimately true or not is indistinct from you perceiving it to be true.

This is true in business. How many deals have you lost based mainly on a subconscious prejudgment of others? You may not know why, but you just don't like the person and so the deal falls through. Networking events are a perfect example of this.

Many people huddle around those with whom they are comfortable and those who do not step out of their comfort zone to meet someone else can lose money.

REALITY IS NOT BASED ON TRUTH, BUT WHAT WE PERCEIVE TO BE TRUE!

Read that again.

We've learned that our reactions to our past, present, and future experiences are not based on an objective truth, but what we perceive to be true.

Let's say you and I are best friends. You've been depressed for quite some time. Nothing in life is going well, your business is on the brink of closing, and you're overwhelmed with problems. So, you buy a lottery ticket in the hope of changing your life. You're lying on your favorite couch in front of the TV awaiting the results.

Then the numbers are read and you realize you are the BIG WINNER. You just won $100 million!

What would you do? Would you lie there and call me with a mopey voice like Eeyore and say, "Hi. How are things? Okay. I just won $100 million. Yeah. It's okay. I thought maybe you would want to come over for a little bit to celebrate ... but not long ... I don't feel well and want to go to bed."

Or would you be jumping around screaming at the top of your lungs, calling me and screaming:

"PHIL! I CAN'T BELIEVE IT! I WON!

I WON ONE HUNDRED MILLION DOLLARS!

GET OVER HERE ... NOW!"

Tremendous energy is exploding out of you as if things are falling off the shelves, light bulbs exploding, wallpaper peeling off the walls. Any feeling of depression, pain, or doom is no longer there and has been overtaken by excitement.

I come over and I can barely open the door. Your energy is like a Category 5 hurricane. I finally get the door open and I'm ducking at the chaos of your excitement. You're like Snoopy—dancing around, screaming at the top of your lungs.

But I come in with a tear slowly running down my face. You look at me, still dancing, and say, "What's wrong with you?"

I ask you to sit down because I have some terrible news. I just received word that your loved one died in a horrific car accident.

Now what would your state be? Would you still be jumping around, smiling and ecstatic?

No, you would start to feel sick to your gut and uncontrollable tears would be rolling down your face. You'd feel that life would not be the same anymore.

Your depression would surely return. You might feel that the world or God has it out for you and that, even when you win, you just can't win. The depression might be even worse than before.

But after a couple of minutes I look at you and I say, "April Fools! I was just kidding. HA! HA! You should have seen the look on your face! You were happy, then sad, crying, all depressed. Oh man, was that funny!"

Now, after you beat the hell out of me, what's the lesson?

You went from a low to a high and back again, but was it based on truth? Well, that can't be because I was lying. It was based on what you perceived to be true. Even though the lottery ticket may have been a winner, we could imagine a scenario where I buy you a lottery ticket and tell you that you won when you really didn't.

It doesn't matter if it's true or not. It matters if you believe it's true. Outside experiences may affect that belief, but how you act or react is up to you.

Humans get very upset at loss. Customers, employees, sales, a house, a loved one. There's a surprise that something was actually removed from our lives without our consent. We have a subconscious belief that there should never be any losses.

We say, "Why? Why me?" But I ask, "Why not me?"

Who are we not to experience loss? What sort of delusion is it that we feel we should be exempt?

Everything and everyone goes through loss. It is life's rejuvenation period.

Later on, I'll explain how to simply and effectively get rid of what isn't working for you and how to replenish it. This is your autumn. Even the most successful crops pass through autumn. They get rid of the old things no longer working for them. They prune what's draining them of energy. Why keep a dying branch alive? Why drain vital resources from the tree?

I understand that most of us don't think this way. Instead of letting go, we hold tight to dead branches and wonder why our life is in the toilet. We wonder why we wake up tired or feel that life is not fair.

Life is very fair. The only one not being fair is you—by holding onto the people and things that are no longer beneficial. By trying to stop nature from just doing its job. Let go of what is not working and life will appear as fair as it truly is.

Many people think they have no control over this. Some say they do have control. But what's the truth?

Every decision you make, whether in your business or in your personal life, changes your direction. In business, you're faced with countless forks in the road. Do I stay on course or do I deviate?

Some people get analysis paralysis, some make decisions based on gut feelings, while still others stay the course no matter what.

We often forget that we're in the driver's seat. The decision to change or stay on course is up to us. Even though we say at times that "my boss made me do it," or "I had no choice but to follow her lead," or that "you have to do this, or you don't want to know what will happen."

> Your decision to experience or not to experience a particular consequence will determine the degree of your suffering or your happiness.

We choose what we want to do, say, or be – and our decisions result in consequences. Choosing not to go to work may cause a reprimand from your boss or worse. Not eating, depending on how long you keep it up, will kill you.

There are consequences attached to each choice. You are choosing whether or not you are willing to experience the consequence.

"But I have no choice; it MUST be done," you say. I agree. I agree because that is your perception of that situation at that particular time. Why is it that the same scenario in a different context wouldn't have the same "must" attached to it? Because the consequences are not the same.

You choose not to do "that" but do "this" because you did not want to experience the consequence attached to "that."

So, it's not "I can't," but "I won't." It all comes down to your perception of the consequences of what or who you choose to experience.

Your decision to experience or not to experience a particular consequence will determine the degree of your suffering or your happiness.

No one else has the power to choose for us—not our spouse, our parents, our kids, our boss, our customers, our in-laws ... NO ONE! Unless we give them that power.

If you feel you have no control in your life, then you're being controlled by others. Who will you give the power to decide your fate? Will you give it to others or remain in control?

CHAPTER THREE

ARE YOU WILLING TO PAY THIS PRICE FOR SUCCESS?

Once upon a time, there was a fairy called The Fairy That Wanted More. This fairy seemed to be ordinary. At least, that's how the fairy felt and so the other fairies treated it that way. It would wake up every morning and go through its morning ritual without thinking and flap its wings to go off to work in the garden.

Some days it would see itself emotionless in the mirror. Other days it would look and dream of a different and more exciting life. But that dream would slip into the World of Never.

See, this World of Never isn't visible to anyone or anything. But it's all around us waiting to envelope our hopeful dreams. Your thoughts trap those dreams and keep them from ever escaping.

"I am never going to get that raise. I will never meet the 'one.' Who am I to even think of a better life? There will never, ever be a chance for me to achieve my dreams."

So the fairy went on with life. At times it would revisit its dreams, but over time that feeling faded until its disbelief sent every dream to the World of Never. Before long, the fairy became pale and sad. And its wings shriveled up and soon it couldn't fly at all.

You may feel wingless. Like nothing you're doing is bringing you closer to materializing your dreams. But I have good news. It doesn't have to be that way. Thankfully, there's a simple way for you to understand why this is happening along with a simple solution.

Your potential is so powerful that it overwhelms you. You are not unsuccessful because you think you can't. You are unsuccessful because you know you can and it scares the hell out of you.

Those of you who make a lot of money are very successful at being rich. Those of you who don't are very successful at being poor. Correct? Would you agree?

However, I would be as correct to say that those of you who make a lot of money are not only successful at being rich but equally as unsuccessful at being poor. Likewise, those of you who are successful at being poor are also just as unsuccessful at being rich.

Something similar could be said of weight loss. If you feel you failed to reach your goals, what's happened is that you're successful at being overweight. A new patient of mine explained to me her weight loss failures during a nutritional consult. She explained how she became a diabetic, was always in pain, and wanted to do something about it.

I sat down, looked her right in the eyes, and congratulated her on becoming a successful overweight, depressed, sluggish diabetic. Congratulations were in order for someone who worked as hard as she did at her success. She was very good at it and could teach others how to do the same thing. Needless to say, she looked at me in disbelief.

I said this to show her that she was not a failure. She had the potential to change these behaviors. She was very successful—depending on how she looked at it. I wasn't being mean, but wanted to shock her into seeing her potential.

Throw yourself into her place for a minute. Could you teach that subject just as well? How about teaching someone how not to make a quota? Not to write a book? Not to make money? Not to have a consistent flow of customers? How to be fearful of change?

I told her that if she didn't want that to be her success story any longer she would have to think, act and be different. She would have to change. Which would mean she'd have to eat differently, drink differently, take nutrients that would start her healing phase and exercise on a regular basis. She'd have to listen to others who have a totally different viewpoint. She'd have to meditate and tap into the supply of health within her and not the dis-ease. She would have to eliminate from her circle of friends and family those who refused to support her and those who would slow her down in her quest for health, wealth, and happiness.

That scared the hell out of her. The true cause of not realizing your dreams and desires is that it's less scary to stay where you are than it is to make changes.

Most people wait until the pain of their present circumstance becomes more painful than changing. That's how people end up in my office.

It's the same with my business clientele. Until your current state is more painful than the perceived pain of hiring a consultant or simply changing your behavior, you won't take action.

I can even predict the future! Until the pain of continually doing what made you successful becomes more painful than a new strategy, you'll end up right back where you started.

My patient knew that she had the potential to achieve her dream of being healthy. She knew she could become unsuccessful at being a diabetic, but first she needs to change her perception.

Of course, this didn't happen all at once. It took her years to accomplish these symptoms and this disease and she was perfecting it every day. Why wouldn't she take the same effort to change? But she gave it her all and now she's good at it.

To reiterate, we are unsuccessful because we know we can do it and it scares us. It's not the goal that we set which scares us but the price we must pay to achieve it.

Do you want a better life? What do you have to give up in order to get it? Do you want that promotion, to make more sales, to get more customers? What price do you have to pay for it?

Is it to spend less time with your family—like Beverly had to? Do you have to go back to school or get new training? Maybe you have to change jobs or finally open your own company?

The old saying rings true: you must give before you receive. You need to create a void within you so that something else can occupy that space that you and you alone have created. You're in control every step of the way.

Have you ever started thinking positively and then, seemingly from nowhere, life spirals out of control and things aren't going well at all? Well, where do you think you will put that positive thinking once it comes in if you don't have room for it? Something else has to go first. You can hold onto pain or you can hold onto happiness, but never both at the same time. Let go of one and you can grab onto and make space for the other.

Many chronic pain patients don't get better because they do not want to let go of the pain. Some use the pain to give their power over to others where usually they feel powerless. The pain may get them the sympathy they wouldn't usually get if they didn't have it. Their pain is their partner, their friend. Food is a friend to some. Cigarettes, drugs, sex and alcohol are friends because they numb the pain. All of these addictions give us an excuse for not achieving our goals and reaching our full potential in life.

Why do you think you can't seem to earn money? Why is it that, when money does come to you, new bills come with it? It's because if you had the money you'd have to do the very thing you've been dreaming about and that kind of success scares us or feels unattainable. The money would eliminate your excuse.

I have another patient named John. John owned his own business. He was overweight and just getting by. As he went through my program he started to lose the weight, people were complimenting him, and he started to increase his income. Then, as it often happens with every patient, he hit a wall.

He started to slowly gain back the weight, business declined, and as a result he was becoming depressed again.

That imaginary wall was his comfort zone. What he was doing was less painful than reversing the trend and feeling comfortable.

What we were able to ascertain together was that he had reverted back to his old self not because what he was doing was painful and he was getting bored, but because success for him was represented by his successful father, whom he despised and told himself he would never become. He associated financial success with doing harm to others, his family, or himself. And the compliments he was getting caused him to feel that, if he didn't continue that road to success, he would end up looking like a failure to all.

Once he was able to provide his own reasons for spending and making money outside of what his father had done with his, then and only then was he able to pass through his comfort zone to become "comfortable being comfortable."

In her book, *A Return To Love*, Marianne Williamson says:

> Our deepest fear is not that we are inadequate.
> Our deepest fear is that we are powerful beyond measure.
> It is our light, not our darkness that most frightens us.
> Your playing small does not serve the world.
> There is nothing enlightened about shrinking so that other people
> Won't feel insecure around you.
> We were all meant to shine as children do.
> It isn't in some of us, it's in everyone.
> And as we let our own light shine
> We unconsciously give others permission to do the same.
> As we are liberated from our own fear
> Our presence automatically liberates others."

So, what is really stopping you from experiencing your destiny? Well, how can you know what's stopping you without fully understanding the players and rules of the game?

Let me share with you a profound discovery I made. The discovery that is the blueprint of nature's repeatable success.

SECTION 1 SUMMARY

1. In reviewing all my past experiences, am I able to acknowledge that my perception of each experience at that time, molded who I am today?

2. What untruths do I still believe are holding me back in my business and my personal life?

3. What painful actions am I avoiding that are stopping me from achieving my goals?

SECTION 2: INTRODUCING NATURE'S BLUEPRINT

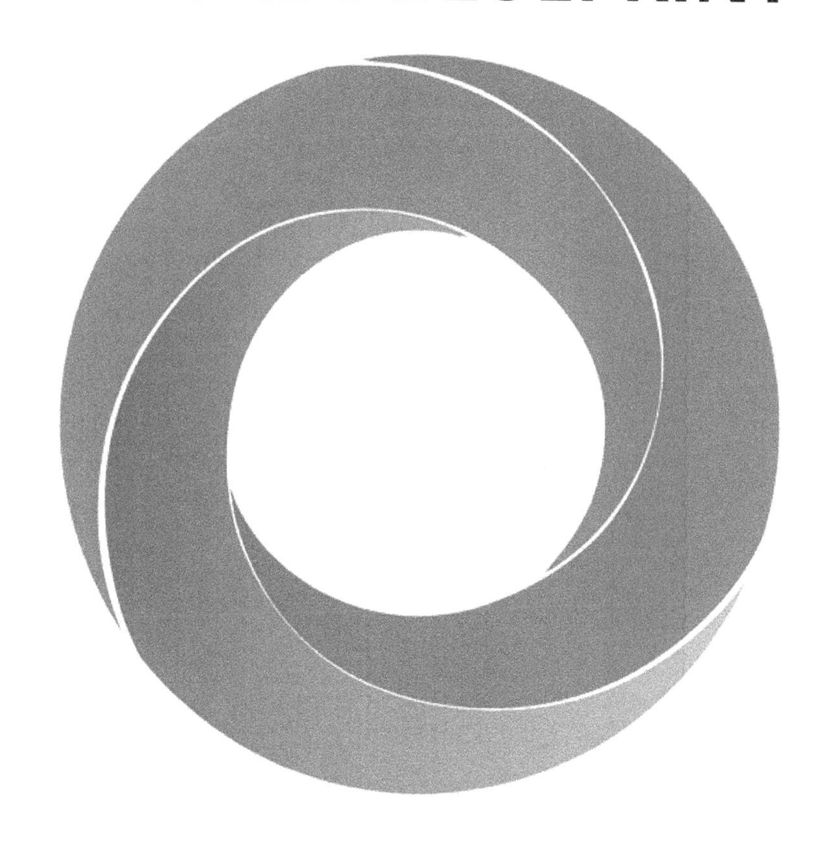

CHAPTER FOUR

How Nature's Blueprint Was Discovered

Have you ever been asked by a rose bush to help it create roses? How about a tree asking for help changing the color of its leaves? No?

What would happen if you had to remember to wind up your heart or remember to breathe or make sure your food gets digested? You definitely wouldn't have much time to read!

So what do the rose bush, tree, and your body know that you don't?

I am going to share a secret I discovered that will show you the blueprint of how nature succeeds year after year without our help.

In the late 1980's, I met a woman named Emily Knight. She was a patient of mine who opened my eyes to the world of meditation and life's spirituality. She told me that a guided meditation would help me understand some of the barriers I had put up. I was skeptical but intrigued, so I gave it a go. The experience of that session was profound and I was hooked and wanted to know more.

Emily and her husband, Dennis, and I had many conversations. Those conversations gave me insight to look at the world in a way that I never knew existed.

In 1991, through this process, Emily and I slowly discovered that our lives were mimicking the four seasons. Each season had a relevant meaning and everybody and everything appeared to follow their cycle. As a result, we started to present seminars, which we called The Seasons of Your Life: Finding Answers Within. This two-day seminar consisted of two meditations and exercises to understand the meanings of the seasons.

Participants would then be taught precisely how the seasons affected their lives.

Despite the success of the seminar, a few years later, our careers took us in separate directions. But I was fascinated, and tirelessly continued to research the seasons. Before long I noticed that not everything could be explained by these four seasons alone—especially color.

We are taught there are three primary colors. Since three doesn't go into four (as in seasons) and so three primary colors couldn't relate to anything but three. But what about their complementary colors? Now I had six colors and I couldn't explain them with the four seasons either.

But one day when I was laying on my bed thinking about all of this, to my amazement, I suddenly realized there aren't four seasons but six.

I won't bore you with exactly how it took two and half decades to fully understand this. All I can say is that after countless hours of talking to thousands of patients, friends, and family about how they themselves and the lives around them followed the course of these six seasons, and how these seasons affected everything from the atoms to the galaxies, I knew without a doubt that my theory was correct.

I want to share with you how this blueprint enabled me to find three basic principles of the universe—affecting everything from your business to your earnings, from your family dynamic to your health. But, as with any profound knowledge, what I cover here won't show the whole picture.

The information in this book is just the tip of the iceberg of what I discovered. There is much more that I am not sharing for good reason. In the past, when I gave all of the information at once, it was confusing and overwhelming.

The point of this book is to use what I've learned to show you why you aren't succeeding and how the information I provide can help you change that. If you'd like to know more beyond this book, you can go to www.dragrios.com. You can use the programs I've developed as well as personal consultations, to individualize this to your life, your business, or your career. I've seen the most successful results come from working together.

But, before we dive deep into the knowledge ahead, it's important for you to remember that I've learned from years of experience--this can and has helped people in their personal lives and businesses. The technique I developed to help my patients heal carried over to their business lives and the improvement was always dramatic.

Now let's take a look at Nature's Blueprint for Repeatable Success for your life and business!

CHAPTER FIVE

UNDERSTANDING NATURE'S BLUEPRINT

Why do you hire consultants, buy online courses or go to seminars? Because you are looking for proven ideas and plans – blueprints – to be successful without having to always figure things out yourself. This saves time and money and allows you to focus on your creativity, management and growth of your business, and many times, affects your personal life.

> To see the most successful blueprint of all time, just look outside your window.

If you want to see the most successful blueprint of all time, just look outside your window. Nature has been using it and it has been hidden right in front of us - until now.

This chapter will give you the basis of the blueprint. I must warn you--this is not all of the blueprint. The entire blueprint goes much more in depth. However, I wanted to give you the simplest form and will share the rest of it in future books and courses.

As I explained earlier, I discovered that there are really six seasons and not the four we know so well. There is a very important reason to know and understand this concept, which I will explain in the chapters ahead. First, let me review the following diagram with you.

(Note: you can go to www.dragrios.com/images to see this in color. Each season has a different color in order for you to get a better grasp of the changes from season to season.)

The cycle of the six seasons is shown below:

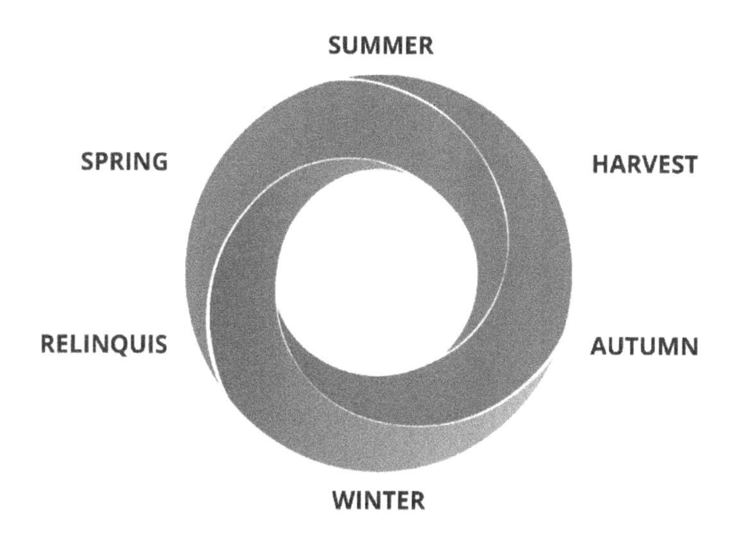

As you can see in the diagram, the two additional seasons I've called harvest and relinquis.

When it pertains to nature itself, each season lasts around two months. For the Northern Hemisphere, summer months are June and August; harvest – September and October; autumn – November and December; winter – January and February; relinquis – March and April and spring – May and June. For those of you who live in the Southern Hemisphere, reverse the months for each complementary season (i.e. winter in the Southern Hemisphere is July and August, and summer is January and February).

Please remember nature does not have a definitive day separating one season from another. There is always a transition period wherein characteristics of each season meld until the demarcation is apparent. The dates given here relate to the meaning of each season but are not exact.

Now that we have this in front of us, how can this blueprint explain, inform, and improve our lives? But before we get to that, let's start with the example of a tree.

In summer, the tree is healthy and fully bloomed. Summer is the production season and so the tree produces what it's here to create. What it creates is the knowledge that lies within the fruit. By biting into the fruit, you receive the knowledge and understanding of its potential. If it is sweet, then it can be eaten or sold. If it is bitter, then a different decision will be made for its destiny.

The fruit on the vine is of no use to anyone unless you simply like looking at apples. By biting into it, you find the nutrients that cause the body to grow.

This is what your business is here for -- to cause growth. Even if you are a demolition company, you have caused growth by creating space.

It's the same for us. For the product, service or life that we have created, we need to decide what we want to do with it once we ascertain its main purpose. This is the assessment needed to be made in summer. If no decision is made, then nature will take over and give you the results for the next season.

This is why summer is the time for decisions. You choose what to do from past knowledge and understanding which creates your reality, your product. The tree took the same path. Its reality is the apples that were created by the nutrients in the soil combining with the inner workings of the tree.

Harvest follows and is a time to replenish by gathering what nature produced. This replenishment allows you to sustain or weather out any future storms or problems that are heading your way. Let's say, for example, that our tree is an apple tree.

During harvest we gather the fruit that is ready to be eaten and the tree gathers or absorbs. Chlorophyll (the substance that makes the leaves green) stops being produced and the tree soaks up all the energy it would have used on chlorophyll to save for winter. During the harvest, nature gathers and conserves what it needs to survive. It accepts and receives the energy that it once gave in order to self-nourish itself so later it can nourish others. If it does not replenish at this time, it will have a hard time to survive and prosper.

Next comes autumn. This is the season of detachment or breakdown. The tree creates a barrier of cells called the abscission layer. Abscission means cutting or severing. The tree literally disconnects itself so no chlorophyll (and so no energy) is supplied to the leaves. This is why we sometimes call autumn, fall. The leaves detach from the tree and eventually fall to the ground. Likewise, autumn is when the leaves start to be broken down by fungus, water, and our trampling feet. During that process the tree is ensuring its later replenishment as nutrients are placed back into and stored in the soil.

Winter is the storage season. The tree has stored its energy in its branches and trunk and so is typically able to survive the winter. Trees that keep their leaves, like evergreens, slow their energy consumption during this season reflecting the typically shorter days. Many countries engage in daylight savings—storage of time itself.

We typically think that the next season is spring. Spring is actually the growth season, but, before anything is grown, there is a very important step that I call relinquis.

Winter has stored potential, or hidden, energy. In relinquis, the process of relinquishing whatever that has been stored in winter begins. This season releases the potential energy to a form which now can be utilized for growth. The water trapped as ice is released to supply the tree and the warming soil begins to relinquish its nutrients. The tree starts to circulate chlorophyll to begin the process of budding. During relinquis, winter's storage lid is lifted to allow this unpacking for spring.

Relinquis can also be thought of as the surrendering or emergent season. Bears emerge from their dens, birds release their songs to break the silence of winter, and seeds and flowers are exposed, ready for pollination.

We all know this: a tree can bud all it wants but it won't get very far without pollination. Nothing grows until something is connected to pollinate the bud to allow for growth. Hence the saying, "April showers bring May flowers." Relinquis exposes the bud or seed of the tree so it can be pollinated.

Pollination is the transfer of pollen to a stigma, flower, ovule or plant to allow fertilization. This process is typically carried out by insects, wind, water, and birds—the pollinators of the world.

Spring is connection. It's the growth season and for anything to grow, you need connection, like that of a bee to a flower. The bee touches the flower while the pollen sticks to it so the bee can spread it around and the world becomes vernal and lush. Our apple tree, since it doesn't have legs and can't move, relies on outside sources such as these for survival and growth. What is given or surrendered in relinquis is reconnected anew in spring.

And then we return to summer—the production season. This is the fruit of the labor of the tree throughout this entire cycle. This season allows the tree to provide shade, protection for birds and other animals, and to produce the fruit which sustains life. Summer is also the wholeness or completeness season. It brings the whole of nature to light.

This cycle maintains regardless of precisely when the necessary seasonal change comes. If the seasons cycled completely over the course of a month, it'd be hard for the tree to adjust as well as it normally would, but the cycle follows the blueprint no matter what. Time will always force summer to bow to harvest and the process goes on unchanged.

You may be thinking that a forest at the equator doesn't experience certain seasons or the ice at Antarctica. On the contrary, they do. No matter where you are on this earth, they all happen. Maybe not at the degree or length that you are used to, but they do occur. If not, the forest at the equator would be miles high if no breakdown was occurring and only growth.

Also, I did not split two seasons merely to think I discovered something cool. You will see later in this book, how out of these six seasons, three basic principles are created to govern everything from the atoms to the galaxies.

Now that you understand how the living things in nature benefit from this cycle, let me explain how you can maximize this benefit for your business and your life.

CHAPTER SIX

OUR BLUEPRINT FOR REPEATABLE SUCCESS

The tree innately knows Nature's Blueprint and does not fight this natural cycle. It does not resist the progression of the seasons, trusting them in order to be fruitful year after year. We as humans also inherently follow the seasons but, because of our ability to control our decisions based on thoughts and feelings, we can resist these seasonal changes causing havoc and stress and decreasing our chances for a fruitful life.

I'd like to show you exactly how we follow the same cycle of seasons. With this knowledge, you can understand why in the past you have made the decisions which caused you both beneficial and detrimental consequences and how to simply change them for the future.

IMPORTANT NOTE: As I explained earlier, nature changes these seasons approximately every two months. However, when they pertain to your business and life, you don't have to wait for nature to change them. You can do it immediately or take as long as you like.

The example I'm about to share with you will show how my patient became aware of how her own seasons were affecting her business and life. They gave her the insight that her actions created a certain season and by knowing how to take advantage of that seasonal insight, she was able to move through the cycle and change her outcomes.

When I say she was in a particular season, it doesn't mean she was in the season that was being experienced outside in nature, but the season within her behavioral pattern. Your own personal seasons affect everything, from the success or failure of your business to successes and failures in your life. The timeline of your seasons can be seconds, months, years, or even decades. You may be in the season of autumn at work and spring in your personal life, or be in summer in both. You can have five deals going on the same time and each one is in a different season. Let's take a look at how Karen was able to use her seasons for the outcomes she desired.

Karen was a commissioned salesperson, married with children, and a patient of mine. She came to me due to an autoimmune thyroid condition called Hashimoto's Disease. She was overweight, tired, losing her hair, had gut issues and brain fog—just to name a few symptoms. As you can imagine, she was extremely stressed out.

She started with my autoimmune program and her condition improved, and soon we began to work on the personal mentoring aspect of the program. She told me one of the reasons for her stress was that her health was affecting her income. Illness affected her motivation to sell and, since she was working on commission, she lost plenty of potential sales. Throughout the mentoring, we looked closely at every aspect of her life—both what was working and what wasn't.

Thoroughly dissecting her process helped us to discern her options. This is what you would do if you were looking after that apple tree personally. You would ascertain whether or not the fruit was sweet or bitter. If it was sweet, you would continue doing the same things you did last year. If the fruit was bitter, you would do things differently. You'd make a necessary change. Perhaps you'd provide different soil, nutrients, or whatever you thought the tree needed to produce sweeter fruit. You may be able to better protect the tree from its environment. You examine the produce of summer so you can begin understanding what needs to be done for your following season – harvest.

Using the season of summer, Karen looked at her sales and realized, due to her environment of sickness and stress, she needed to change. I asked her key summer questions, "What you have produced so far in your business and in your life, does this work for you? Does this make you anything but satisfied? If not, then are you ready to decide to change?"

Once she saw that the fruit of her labor was bitter, we used harvest to gather the information she needed to understand clearly what was working in her life and what wasn't. It was time for her to say NO to others so that she could replenish herself since she overly gave in relinquis and did not take enough in her previous harvest.

Harvest is the desire whether or not to tolerate what was produced in summer. Her decision in summer was to no longer allow this type of fruit to be produced which caused her bitterness toward life. This conclusion was reinforced by examining what she was giving and receiving and how this affected her personal and business relationships.

My question to her was, "What will you keep in your life and how will you nurture yourself differently?"

Harvest is self-nourishing, self-replenishing. It stops giving or supplying and lessens excessive generosity, so you can take what's needed for yourself. Unfortunately, this is often mistaken for being selfish.

I want you to read this next sentence three times:

Self-nourishment does not equal selfishness.

The difference is subtle, so I think it's worthwhile to spend just a few minutes talking about it.

Many people can't stand selfishness. They never want to be viewed as selfish, so they overcompensate and give too much. They wouldn't dare to take for themselves.

Let's say you're one of these people. You give away your time, and your emotional energy. You are exploited at work. You take on extra hours with no compensation or praise. You give your services away for free. You'd never want to be called selfish! But—what's left for you? How will you make overhead? Where's your raise or promotion? Sleep—what's that? Whose shoulder is offered up when you need comfort? All your time is spent giving to others and nothing is left to take for yourself.

> Self-nourishment does not equal selfishness.

The apple tree certainly doesn't do that. Its giving is gradual. Others take from it, but it always takes for itself in some way: through sunlight, water, and allowing autumn to break down the leftover fruit, branches and leaves to turn them into nutrients for a fertile soil.

You are not being selfish when you do things for yourself and say no to others. Especially to people who take without ever giving. But being too stingy just turns you into Scrooge. Those who hold onto things and do not share, slowly wither and are usually alone. Their winter energy runs out. And for those who give too much, there will come a time when there will no longer be anything left to give. Nothing can be harvested.

The key is always a balance between what's given and what's taken. Extremes cause the same result—a slow withering away. Karen took the time to gather new information from me, said no to others who were draining her energies, and started to nourish herself as best as she could. Once she took what she needed, she moved into autumn. She needed to disconnect from those people, things, and events that were no longer conducive to the new fruit she wanted to bear. She looked at demanding clients and realized how she had become less productive and knew she needed to fire them. She also knew she needed to fire her own ways of communicating with her clients, co-workers, and boss.

It was time to clean house and start fresh.

She then moved into winter. It was time for her to meditate. To go within, where wisdom is held. The wisdom of winter is deep within the forest and the clear branches allow us to see it. It was time for her to be still, frozen, to assess the potential energy that was waiting to be tapped into.

Winter is the planning stage, the re-sequencing of steps you want to take to grow sweeter fruit. Therefore, we need quiet and stillness, to turn off any electronic gadgets, and be at peace. We need to disconnect from others in autumn to move into winter. This is where the true imagination and inspiration of genius comes from. Winter stores all of our potentialities, waiting for the season of relinquis to release them. Knowledge is not power, only the potential for power. That potential requires action if it's to be worth anything.

Once you have a plan and the clarity received in winter, your envisioning of what you want your future summer or produce to look like, relinquis will take over. Relinquis is your internal execution. The flower needs to start its internal movement to open the bud. You need to take your plan of winter and start executing it, too.

This is your desire to unfold your plans so they can be shown to the world. You can have all the clarity you want, but if you don't have the burning desire to implement it, you can't melt the barrier of ice to release the water which will nurture your plans.

You must surrender to that desire. Through surrendering, which is a form of giving, you open up so the world can see, hear, and feel what you are asking for. You let go of the barrier that contains your plans.

This is where, especially with religious doctrine, you must surrender or die of the flesh to be reborn. That can be scary. However, what is really meant is to surrender the protective barrier that you have created and allow the world to see your true potential of winter. It can be misinterpreted that you are going to lose something precious and perish. No! You are losing the defensive wall you built so nothing can get in or out -- whereby you slowly perish instead of using the true power of relinquis.

Winter's clarity and relinquis' desire allow you to start the attraction phase. The law of attraction is the season of relinquis. You're attracting the bees that will pollinate you. The bees are the people and things that will come to you to help you realize your future goals.

Are you killing your bees or allowing them to pollinate your flowers? Once you are clear and you have a burning desire, then and only then can you go into to spring to connect with others and start growing.

Impatience is common in relinquis as it starts its transition into spring. You might get angry and say, "I have been working hard and I see nothing coming to fruition." You don't immediately see the fruit, the people and things, the opportunities that are in front of you. But they're there, regardless.

If you had that apple tree in your backyard, would you chop it down because you only saw flowers? Of course not. You would nourish it and make sure it had what it needed to produce the fruit in summer.

When impatience sets in, remember that you're in relinquis, not in summer. This is where people often abandon their ideas. They don't see that the opportunities that were always right in front of them, just needed time to be connected with their pollinators. They needed to move into spring to spark growth.

Karen took the clarity she obtained in winter and felt excited for the first time in a very long time. Her desire to meet her goals started to nourish her clear plan.

Then, once she had the desire, it fueled her into action to start connecting and changing her communication as she'd planned. She now moved into spring. It was time to connect with her pollinators – her boss, clients and potential clients.

She connected with her boss to get permission to fire those demanding clients and was able to show him how they were causing a decrease in productivity. We discussed what sort of client she wanted and she started to attract them.

She said, "They were coming out of nowhere!" I said, "No, your clear plan combined with your desire allowed you to connect with your 'bees'. Your spring started to grow your business in the direction you wanted."

Then came the best part—summer. Her fruit – both her personal and professional life – became sweeter. People were now viewing her new tree, her new business and personal life and how it was being presented.

Karen was even able to keep some of her previously demanding clients. They became less demanding because she no longer tolerated their ways. The tides changed and they did not want to lose her so they bloomed into her ideal clients. Once she communicated differently and gave them what she was willing to give, they changed according to her plan. Others were let go and quickly replaced ten-fold. The universe abhors a vacuum, and she had a very clear plan for who would fill the gaps.

As for Karen's general health, the timeframe for healing was longer. But the seasons maintained their blueprint for success and with a clear plan, a desire to carry it out, a surrender of control, and patience, she improved. She then was able to move into harvest where she was getting paid, replenishing her stores, not only in monetary gains but in health and happiness. However, Karen would have never received these insights or her ability to change if she did not view her past “failures” as essential for growth.

Your new knowledge of the seasons can give you the next step in any given situation so you too can duplicate Karen’s achievement with Nature's Blueprint For Repeatable Success.

CHAPTER SEVEN

WHY FAILURE IS ESSENTIAL FOR YOUR INSIGHT

In business and in life the "F" word is failure. But is failure as bad as we have been led to believe?

You may have made one of the following statements more than once:

Life is not fair!

It's a tough world.

It's a dog eat dog world out there and it's scary!

You should walk in my shoes. You wouldn't last long.

But the truth is that life has its ebbs and its flows, its expansion and contraction, its life and death. Life is just about contrast. We live in a dichotomous world. Right/left, up/down, in/out. There is an opposite for every action.

Take the villain or villains out of a movie script. Why would you keep watching? Without conflict, there's no motivation for good to triumph. Or think how weird it would be to buy a ticket to a baseball game where only the home team showed up. It would be absurd to spend your hard-earned money on watching a pitcher play catch for an endless inning. It's the contrast, the opposition, that creates our motivation. It seeks out its opposite—success. Failure employs success.

In Chapter 6, I showed you how the seasons create growth and breakdown, spring and autumn.

If fungus didn't grow in the forest, imagine how high the leaves would be piled up. And without the breakdown of leaves, the trees wouldn't get the nutrients they need and they would die. No fruit could possibly grow.

The tree lets go of its fruit not only to feed the outside world, but to nurture itself. It works the same in life. You're in business or in a personal relationship not only to give to others, but also to yourself. It's not selfish because this type of exchange is essential for your business, your relationships, and the world to function healthfully.

> It's the contrast, the opposition, that creates motivation.

Many business professionals view business and personal life as entirely separate. But your business and your personal life are the same thing. They are you.

The workaholic thinks the key to success is to work long hours while everything else suffers. But the balance of contrasts means that for business to be successful, personal life requires more work than neglect. If a person works less on business endeavors and more on family and friends making sure time is evenly distributed to both, then the business not only is more satisfying, but also increases. This will lead to reduced stress and the person will be less vulnerable to poor decision-making and more willing to take the risks necessary to grow. The end result is a more balanced life. I've seen this time and time again—both with my patients and myself.

This was one of the many reasons that led to my divorce. I was taught by my father to make sure I provided for my family. It was very important—more important than being with them. I know now that this was what he was taught as a boy. I see the countless hours I missed with my daughters when they were growing up, the missed opportunities, all because of my perception that it was what I was supposed to do. I thought that was a father's job.

I made sure I had people in my world who reinforced that belief as well and they were just as miserable as I was. Once I realized it didn't have to be the case, I changed my inner thinking, thereby changing my outer world.

My failures allowed me to awaken my insight. If I focus on the failures and how horrible a business person I am or the humiliation I feel, then I do not focus on the greatest gift it is giving me – wisdom and innovation.

One of the greatest gifts you can give yourself is to make a mistake. This way you know if you are on the right path or not.

It's finding the balance between making a rash decision and having indecision. Giving yourself the time to think it through but letting go of taking too much time. Experience is the deciding factor. Having the experience of both decisions allow you to find the middle road.

If Thomas A. Edison, who had 1,093 patents for different inventions, had given up because of the various "failures" that went along with his innovations, they would have been discovered by someone else and his name would have never been known. In fact, he famously noted to his associate, Walter S. Mallory, "I have gotten lots of results! I know several thousand things that won't work!"

It's important for you to see there are two actions we do every day: we are either giving or receiving, open or closed, growing or shrinking, building or destroying, expanding or contracting, opening or protecting — to name a few. Pick a word that relates to your current problem or success and its corresponding opposite.

As Edison was "failing," he was innovating. He was in a sense, vibrating. He was sending out ideas and experimenting as well as receiving the answers he needed to find the path that led to his solution.

You may have heard of the concept that we are vibrational beings or that your vibration is very important. This is not a mystical idea but a scientific one. What is vibration? It is the expansion and contraction of energy. Expansion and contraction are also growth and protection; highs and lows; sending out and bringing in; giving and receiving. It's the excitement resonating from you. Are you being attuned to the answer that is coming back? It must come back -- and it is your interpretation that will determine whether it is a failure, a success or merely information.

It doesn't matter what you call it (after all, it is just words), but what you feel from it is what matters. Your feeling determines the flow in which people, things and events come into and out of your life.

That's it. From the atoms to the galaxies, we are only committing two actions and they are complete opposites. And they're happening at the same time.

For example, take any nearby object. Take this book. Put the book in front of you with one of your hands behind it. Now move the book toward your nose. As you bring it closer to you, would you say that the book is coming toward you? Yes, of course. Is it also moving away from your hand? Yes, of course. Depending on how you see you in relation to the book, you'll get two completely different answers. Depending on your focus – your perception – your answers will vary.

When business is slow or being dismantled, you get upset without ever thinking that it's simply the course of the seasons. But that's like being upset when your body is dismantling the food you just ate in order to absorb the nutrients. Are you upset your heart contracts to pump blood out of it and then expands with blood to be refilled? How about your lungs expanding and contracting? As you take a deep breath in, your lungs expand because your diaphragm contracts. And as a business contracts, the opportunity to deal with conflict expands.

There is a hidden synonymity in success and failure, an expansion of customers one month and a decrease in another. We experience the "negative" because we reach a capacity. All of nature, even the nature of a particular business, recognizes a deficit in another aspect of life and needs to correct the imbalance.

You may think that you can handle a doubling of your business. However, external outcomes show you differently.

This is why it often seems more painful or detrimental for you or your business to expand. You may have to work longer hours and bring in more employees, but are shirking from it because in the past more employees meant more problems. It was more painful to have a bigger business and more money coming in than it was to have fewer employees and the comfort you associated with that state. Instead of embracing the decrease, the contraction, the successful failure, you've now reached your limits and are being externally regulated. And nature makes no mistakes.

A lack in your life is never a bad thing, but is actually more comfortable and important than bringing in what you desire before you're ready. There is no one way street to success.

Failure is a gift from life and acceptance gives happiness in return.

When something "negative" happens to me, I rub my hands together like a mad scientist and think, "I wonder what gift I'm getting?" When you focus on the solution or are being grateful for the gift that is coming, then you connect with the solution. You can't focus on the problem since they are the opposite of each other.

An illustrative example I give my patients is putting my hand up with the palm facing them and asking if they can see the back of my hand. They respond with a resounding, "no." Then, I turn the back of my hand toward them and ask if they can see the palm of my hand. Again—a resounding "no." The back of my hand represents the solution and the palm of my hand is the problem. Turning my palm reveals the back of my hand. Just shifting my perception to focus on the solution or potential solution made the problem disappear.

Let's say you worry about money all the time. Then, you win $100 million in the lottery. Do you continue to worry about money? Or do you relax and trust your check is coming soon?

The same applies to any fear. If you trust the solution to your problem is coming, then you can no longer feel fear directly and your energy changes. But if you don't trust it's coming, then you must feel fear.

If you can trust that your business is in autumn and that you must remove what is no longer working, then you must be in spring in another aspect of your business or your life. It's like saying you are the earth experiencing autumn in the Northern Hemisphere but the Southern Hemisphere is not experiencing spring.

Once you can accept that autumn is your solution, you can enter winter to replan your strategy. From there, your desire, your relinquis, will come naturally. You will attract people who reinforce your new plan, since your clarity and desire are so strong. As those seasons are occurring so are their opposites at the same time. It's law. They must happen and, as I've seen with my patients, they do every time.

Look at each problem and ask, "I wonder what gift I am getting?" Reinforce it at every turn. Say it out loud – over and over – until you start to believe it. And watch it manifest.

Three Reasons for Underproduction

Here's how you can be clear about what is causing your underproduction:

1. You are not giving the proper amount of attention and nutrients needed to grow. Perhaps you are spending too little time with clients, or not enough time with family, and this is starting to affect other aspects of your business. Remember to maintain a balanced production.

2. You are not properly protecting your produce from the elements. Make sure that whatever in your life doesn't align with your strategy won't derail you from your production goals. Don't be afraid to let go of people, events, or strategies that will only take up your most precious resource—time.

The tree has died and a new tree needs to be planted. A total failure is nothing but the opening up of new avenues for success. Removal creates space so that something else can be built. Don't hold onto something that only gives you grief or drains you. Business should be a pleasure as well as a challenge, and if the only thing being produced is fireplace kindling, take your gift and move on.

SECTION 2 SUMMARY

1. Nature's Blueprint has six seasons or steps that it uses to create and repair. Nature changes to each season approximately every two months. However, we can utilize them in any time frame and start with any one we choose.

2. Each season has only one job. Understanding and fully utilizing each one maximizes your effort in creating or repairing your end result.

3. Failure is nothing more than an indication that either one or more of the seasons was not applied fully or it implies a

change of direction is needed. Remember, each signal has two opposite meanings. As discussed in the first section, your actions will be determined by whether you perceive it as beneficial or detrimental.

SECTION 3: UTILIZING NATURE'S BLUEPRINT

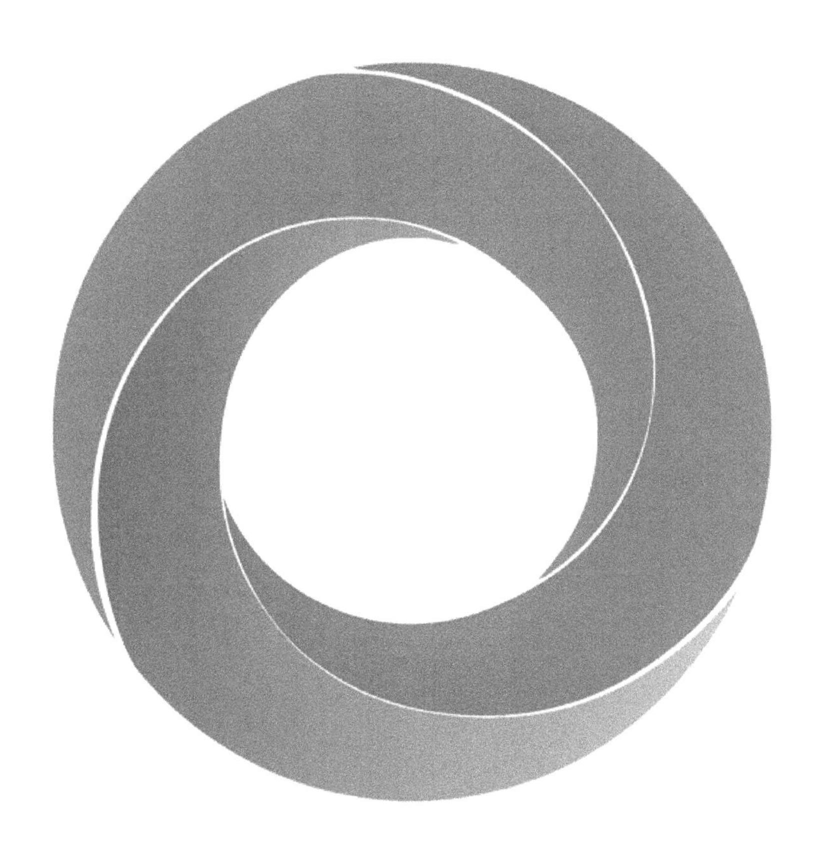

CHAPTER EIGHT

SUMMER – TIME TO DECIDE

For every sense you experience, there is always an opposite thought, feeling, and emotion waiting to emerge from within you. Whether you are sad or happy, angry or loving, you choose the ingredients within yourself to create what you desire.

It is the same with the tree. The ground has all the nutrients it needs to blossom. Even if the soil is barren, the tree's death provides nutrients for the soil at a later time. But, unlike the tree, people can move about and find whatever they need. What either stops or propels us is our decision and desire to protect or grow.

Someone once said to me, "There is nothing you do not have." In other words, there is no such thing as a "lack." I adamantly disagreed at that time. My perception showed me nothing but what I was "lacking." I eventually came to understand what this person meant: even though abundance was not physically present, I was abundant with potentialities waiting to be tapped.

These unseen potentialities within you – your winter – spark the desire of relinquis to connect with spring and become externally present in summer—the season of production.

Take a look at the next diagram. Summer is the external result of your hard work that many do not see. This allows you to examine and appraise whether your effort has paid off.

For example, you may notice a lack in your business and know it is not reaching its full potential, just as you would notice the same for a tree. Maybe you are giving too much of your service away and not receiving ample pay. On the other hand, maybe your service is becoming obsolete because you did not track the trends in your field. Now that you can see what's needed, you can make a decision to change what is necessary to produce a different fruit for the next coming summer. You may need to ramp up production, buy new equipment, obtain new information or protect your product with a patent from those who might exploit it for their own personal gain.

Before I explain the six seasons, I want to point out something very IMPORTANT. You don't need to start with summer. I start here because it is easier to examine what you have created. As you will learn in this book, you can start with either season but for now, until you get more proficient at this, I suggest you start in summer.

SUMMER

This season gives you the ability to view the end result, your product. If you have an apple tree and you bite into the apple, you will need to make a decision. Is the fruit sweet or bitter? Is it to your standards or does it need to be changed?

If it is sweet, then maintain what you did last year and monitor every season. If it is bitter, either cut the tree down or start making changing in every season for a different result.

The same applies to your business and life. With every result, whether a product, service, or relationship , you need to make a decision.

This is why summer is the decision season. What decision? In what direction will I take this product now that I've created it?

The product can be your service, your relationship with someone, or it can be a problem. It's any result that has been created wherein you need to decide what to do with it. If it is fine, then make sure the rest of the seasonal cycle is working the way you know it should. If it isn't to your standards, then it is time to change.

The question you need to ask is, "Am I happy with what has been created or do I need to change this? Is there a problem and am I willing to do something about it?"

How many times you tried to solve something that was never a problem in the first place?

If there is a problem, are you willing to take responsibility for this? Are you willing to do anything about it?

Summer helps define your perception of your situation as truthful or illusory. You may sometimes lie to yourself so you don't really see what a mess you're in. You may think the lie protects you. But you're only protecting yourself from an illusion.

Have you ever tried to make a decision, but realized it was never yours to make? Asking this question reveals whose responsibility it truly is.

Is this really my problem or someone else's? This is a key question because by taking responsibility for someone else's problem has a high chance of failure because you don't own it. If you don't own it, then you have little control in changing it.

Remember, with any decision comes a price. Are you willing to pay that price? If you are committed to do something about it, then you are ready to go into the next season – harvest.

By knowing exactly what is produced in summer and making a decision to change the outcome, you will be better equipped to move into harvest where you take for you.

PLEASE NOTE: I have placed exercises after each season so you can determine what season your business or life is in. I have divided them into personal and business questions to make it easier for you. There are many more questions. However, I wanted you to get a basic understanding of what questions you need to ask for maximal results. My course dives more heavily into these.

For the following exercises to work, you need to be completely honest with yourself and without judgment. Approach this exercise, and all other exercises in this book, as if you are looking at a stranger's business or life and not your own. This way it doesn't become personal, which can skew your honesty.

SUMMER EXERCISES (ASSESSMENT)

BUSINESS QUESTIONS

1. Do our product(s) or service(s) or any other result(s) need to change?

2. Am I able or willing to make a decision regarding my career?

3. Am I willing to take responsibility for this and am I willing to do anything about it?

4. What problem is our business or staff encountering that needs to be addressed?

5. Do we want to solve this problem? If not, why? Are we perceiving more problems will emerge and overwhelm us?

6. Is this problem ours to solve? Is this someone else's and they perceive it to be our problem?

7. Are we as committed to this business as we were when we first started?

8. Is the business going in the right direction? If not, why not?

9. Is the direction of the business where we want or ought to go?

10. Are we clear of the direction that needs to be taken? If not, are we committed to change or do whatever is necessary?

11. Are we properly managing our staff and are they responding in a productive and positive way?

12. Do we have the knowledge to change and the accountability to do so? Do we truly have the knowledge to run our business efficiently and differently if need be?

PERSONAL QUESTIONS:

1. Am I ready to make a change in my life?
2. Does a relationship with a loved one, relative or friend need to be changed?
3. Does any part of me whether on a mental, physical or emotional level need to be changed or improved?
4. Am I willing to take responsibility for what I have created?
5. Is this my problem to solve or someone else's?

CHAPTER NINE

HARVEST – TIME TO PAY YOURSELF

Harvest is known as the end of the growing season and time to gather and store crops. This is also known as early autumn but late autumn as we understand it does something completely different.

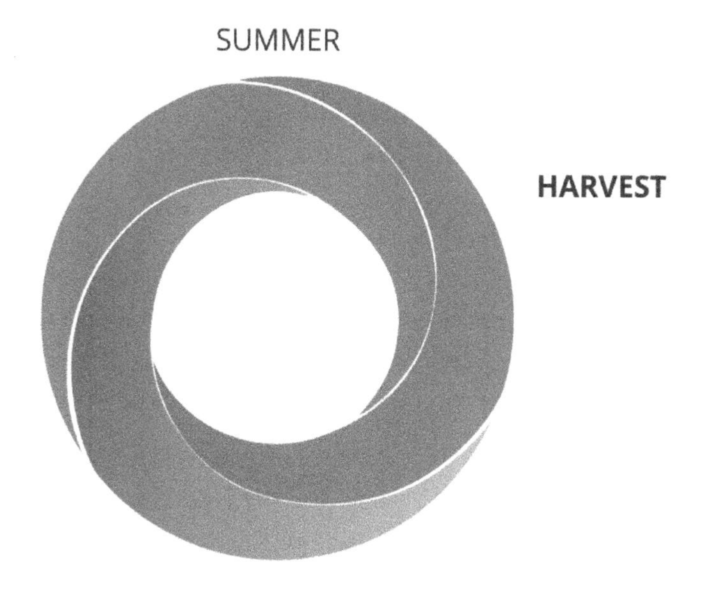

This is the replenishment season. This is the time to take for you, after all the work you did throughout the year growing or creating your product, service or whatever you wanted to manifest in your business and life.

The tree does the same thing in harvest. It stops making chlorophyll to get ready for the winter and replenishes its stores. It stops giving and starts taking for itself. And, if you're tending the tree, you do the same to prepare for the winter. You decide if you're happy with the quality and quantity of your produce or if you'll need to create something different for harvest.

This is when you need to look at your business or your earnings and ask, "Do I make enough? Can I make more with what I have? Does my business need to be tweaked? Or do I have so much debt that people are taking more than I can keep for myself?"

This is why the financial gurus tell you to "Pay yourself first!" I hope you now can see why. The tree does it, why shouldn't you? Harvest is when you get paid. People take your product or service and give you money in return. This is also what happens in relationships, whether with a loved one or your client. This season asks the question, "Is this an even exchange or is it lopsided?"

Harvest is reviewing the values you have gathered throughout your life. Do you feel worthy of love, money, success or whatever you desire at that moment in time? How valuable are you to yourself, your family, your work and society? If you feel that you don't have that much value, then you will gather only what you think you are worth.

Is your product or service not worth your price or is it worth a lot more than what you are selling it for? Are your relationships draining you? I will delve into this much more in depth later in the book when I explain the "negative" effects of harvest as well as the other seasons.

Harvest is your desire for change. Without the desire to change, your decision in summer will be moot. You will go through the seasons and create the same amount as before or maybe even less. If the latter happens, you return to summer with no desire to change and the cycle of underproduction repeats itself.

Why not start desiring to change now rather than wait for it to be so painful? The fear of moving out of your comfort zone is an illusion you create from the evidence of repeatedly poor outcomes. But outcomes only remain poor when you think there is no possibility of changing or if you've lost the ability to desire change. If your perception is rigid and repetitively negative, your outcomes will be as well.

When nothing changes, you might get desperate and start making decisions out of fear. You may have hired a consultant that wasn't for you, added something to your business that really wasn't going to work in the first place, or abandoned a business and become involved in something about which you knew nothing. I've been there.

Following the course of the seasons without resistance will decrease or eliminate the illusion of fear. This will allow you to make different decisions and thereby create different outcomes.

Fear causes you to feel that you are giving without any return on your investment. But you are receiving. Depending on your perception, you can understand the reciprocation that is happening simultaneously. For instance, if you give me a gift without asking for one in return, have you really received nothing? If I accept it, I've given you the opportunity to feel happy, right? That's the joy in giving birthday presents. But, even if I reject your gift, I've given you the opportunity to feel sad. So, no matter what you give, you're always getting something back. These actions happen instantaneously.

Let's say your current outcome, your tree, is ready for harvest and you are not happy with the yield. As a farmer, would you say, "Maybe I'll get lucky next year"? Of course not. You would analyze why:

"Was it due to external forces? From bad weather? If so, did I have a backup plan? Was it that I couldn't afford the right fertilizer and went with a cheaper brand? I don't like harvesting apples, but, because my father did it, I was forced into it? Did I always want to harvest wheat?"

Instead of looking at the negative, that you worked hard but did not produce the yield you hoped for, recognize that you did receive something very valuable. You were given the opportunity or the solution to make your product or service better or abandon it for something more worthwhile. Trust me on this one. In the pursuit of searching for these answers to the seasons, my failures caused me to look somewhere else for the answer instead of what I thought it should be.

Once the true reason is understood, harvest comes if you have a burning desire to change. Are you ready to accept in order to replenish whatever is required? But, beforehand, you need to have the desire to analyze the problem. Focusing on finding a solution is the only way to reverse poor outcomes. You may have wanted to put your head in the sand because it's too painful to know, but with your new understanding of the seasons you can confidently desire and effect change in your life.

Now you've gathered the necessary knowledge to understand the true cause(s) you can begin facing your fear of change.

HARVEST EXERCISES (Replenish)

BUSINESS QUESTIONS:

1. How do I feel about my business or career?

a. Am I getting the rewards, such as money, happiness, sense of fulfillment, etc. that it once gave me? If not, do I believe I can, again?

b. Am I paying myself first?

c. Am I still enjoying the routine and everything that I get from the business? Is this what I signed up for? Do I have the desire to keep doing this? Or am I just burned out and no longer have a desire to be in this business?

d. Am I happy with continuing the business or should I allow the business to close so I can focus on my true desire which is ...

e. If I have a partner(s), board of directors or advisor(s), how is it working and how do I feel about the relationship? Does it need to be improved, and can it?

2. What type of culture did I create here?

a. Am I still proud of the values we stand for and the company we've built?

b. Has the culture (values and business philosophies) become dysfunctional?

c. How do my employees feel about working here?

d. What's my cash flow like? Am I putting enough money away to give my business a healthy marketing budget?

e. Am I hiring high performing employees and paying them well, or do I have underpaid and disgruntled employees?

f. How do employees feel about management and about other employees? Are they feeling valued?

g. Am I and my team service oriented?

PERSONAL QUESTIONS:

What in my life do I need to replenish?

a. Am I worthy of having a healthy, wealthy and happy life?

b. Do I take more than I give?

c. Do I have a hard time saying no to others?

d. Am I overly patient and overly tolerant of others and do not take for myself?

e. Am I impatient and intolerant of others and take too much for myself?

f. How deserving am I to live the life I was meant to live?

g. Do I do whatever it takes to move ahead no matter how many people I hurt?

h. Am I looking for love and acceptance from others because of my inability to love myself?

i. Do I not give enough love and concern to others because I am protecting what little I have within me?

j. Am I no longer receiving the kind of love, respect and/or from any of my relationships whether with loved ones, friends or relatives.

CHAPTER TEN

AUTUMN – TIME TO DETACH FROM WHAT'S NOT WORKING

I call this season autumn even though it is technically late autumn. The reason is many people know autumn as fall. Nature is detaching what is not necessary to prepare for winter. As I explained earlier, harvest and autumn function distinctly and need to be treated as such to truly understand how this blueprint works.

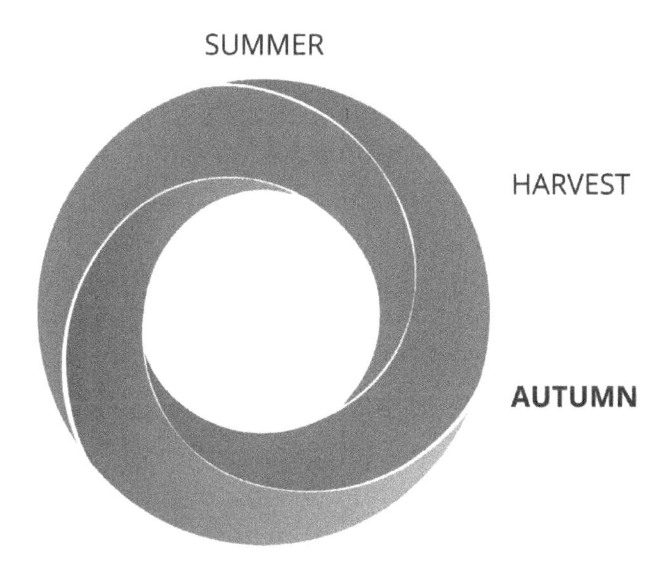

Have you ever wondered what makes the leaves drop? Tree trunks, branches, and twigs can survive the winter, but delicate leaves cannot. At the end of summer, the leaves are filled with sugar. Harvest then allows for the tree to start conserving energy and take for itself.

The cells in the base of each leaf – in what's called the separation layer – start to fill up with a cork-like substance, trapping the sugar in the leaves. Once this happens, water also cannot get to the leaves. With the transition from harvest to autumn, chlorophyll starts to break down with this sequence and the lack of sunlight, causes the disconnection of the leaves from their once life-giving source and breaks them off at the separation layer.

Break down. Separation. Disengagement. Partition. Fracture. This is autumn—the season of disconnection or detachment.

This detachment only occurred due to the previous seasons. In summer, you sensed whether the seasons were successful in creating your perception's ultimate produce by looking at their manifestation. The fruit of summer provided the knowledge needed to understand whether the cycle of the seasons was a success or not.

Then came harvest. This season focused on you. You have everything you need to get out of your state of suffering. Harvest is the time to gather your resources and appraise how much value was gained from summer's produce and what needs to be changed. And all of that change exists in your desire to change your depleting stores.

Once the desire to change appears from within, the transition from harvest to autumn is inescapable.

By releasing the supply that you no longer desire in your life – friends, family, responsibilities, problems, and so on – you create a void, a space between what works and what does not work any longer.

This chapter will show you how to create this space by helping you to decide specifically where the disconnection needs to occur.

However, there is something you really need to understand. Have you ever kept someone or something that was a negative, and everyone told you needed to detach from them? But you couldn't and found reasons to stay or keep the very person or thing that was causing you harm?

The reason is that you did not replenish in harvest and because of this, you'd rather have a negative than nothing. If you gathered what you needed within yourself, you would not be looking outside of you to replenish you.

The next time you feel the unwillingness to detach from someone or something that is causing stress in your life, go back to harvest and revisit the exercises.

Once you feel replenished and the desire to let go of the people and things that are no longer working in your business and your life, then it is time to create a list of detachments.

I call that list The Autumn List. But before we begin, it's important to review three main categories that create our business and life. They go by many names. You may know them as financial, career, social, etc. However, I place them in three categories.

Just remember the Three R's of business and life: Roles, Rewards, and Relationships.

ROLES

Roles are the characters you play, as if your life was a movie and you play every part. What roles do you play in your life? Are you a parent, spouse, aunt or uncle, son or daughter, business owner, volunteer?

Roles deal with your life's direction and responsibilities. They influence your behavior. You may act or even dress entirely differently when playing the role of a mother than when playing the role of, say, a lawyer. With roles come perceived responsibilities and your decisions are affected by those responsibilities and their context. I say perceived because not all those who have the same role will act within society's pre-determined expectations.

Different cultures will dictate different expectations of these roles as well. In one country, a business executive may not be favorably looked upon or viewed as disrespectful if he is ignorant of the customs. An example would be the greeting bow in Japan versus shaking hands in other countries.

Autumn is the season to determine if the present roles you are portraying are what you want to continue to do. I've always had a policy: if it isn't fun anymore, it's time to get out.

When I was just starting my practice, in order to meet people and give back to the town, I was volunteering for many community groups. I created a youth activities committee for the local chamber of commerce. I was doctor for the Pop Warner Football team. In short, I played a lot of roles. At first, I enjoyed every minute of it, but after a few years it was getting out of hand. Some roles which had previously been so enjoyable had become difficult and time consuming. I was no longer having any fun. So I resigned from those groups.

The concept came to me when I had come across a technique that gave me the ability to determine if it was time to stay or move on. I coined it the Time Management Technique. I found it to be powerful in determining exactly how many roles I was playing and how many hours I spent on each per week.

Through this technique, I found I wasn't spending time in the roles I most desired to play. I had become engulfed by my duties and was straying from my purpose.

When I started prioritizing roles I most enjoyed and managing the time I spent with each one, life became more fun and I was much happier.

Below, I outline the Time Management Technique. Take a few moments to complete the exercise and answer each question for yourself.

Time Management Technique

1. Write down all the roles that you play every week: i.e., parent, child, spouse, friend, boyfriend/girlfriend, your career role, service roles such as board or committee member or volunteer, anything that takes time to do. Don't forget to add in SELF as one of these roles for the times when you're on your own. What roles are you playing in your life right now that are not working for you? Are you in a career or a job that you hate? Are you unemployed? Have you volunteered for a position on a board that is taking too much of your time and which you no longer enjoy? Do you want to have a different career? Do you want to be a parent or a spouse? Are you one now? Are you spending too much time in one area and not in enough in another? Do you spend enough time taking care of your needs?

2. Write down the average number of hours per week you spend in each role. Again, do not forget to write down the number of hours you spend by yourself. You can even draw a pie chart to help visualize exactly how much time you are spending in each role.

3. Review the number of hours currently allotted to each role and determine if this is how you want to spend your time every week. You may see that you are spending too many hours on a committee that you no longer enjoy and by quitting you would have time for another role.

4. Eliminate the roles you no longer want, subtracting the number of hours spent on each role from your weekly total.

5. You now have the choice to add time to another role or create a new one. Again, it will be your choice to add personal or alone time to that list.

This technique will help you to redefine the roles you play in your life and to see what is no longer needed or wanted.

REWARDS

Now it's time to review the second 'R'—our Reward system.

You may have been shocked by your results in the exercise above.

We can be rewarded in many different ways: such as with money, or love, or friendship. You may be a millionaire, but are you a millionaire when it comes to love or friends? Rewards are what you supply yourself with based on how valuable you feel you are.

It's important to remember that if you truly desire something, you have to be willing to give up something else in order to achieve it. If you want a better job, more money, a better life, the questions to ask are: What do I have to give up? What price am I willing to pay?, or "What compromises am I willing to make?

It would be absurd to sit in front of a fireplace and say, "Give me heat and then I will give you some wood." Similarly, in life, it's important to give before you can receive. You have to create a void within you so something else – something which you choose and prefer – can occupy it.

Maybe you need to give up your TV, going out drinking, or sitting home feeling sorry for yourself. Maybe you need to start a new degree or pursue a training course so you can get a better job. Want to meet a deadline? Maybe you need to cut out text messaging, video games and computer time and work differently, more often and more thoroughly.

You always have three basic choices: (1) You can throw your life away; (2) You can ignore the people and things causing strife and the stress will transfer to all other aspects of living; or (3) You can remove these people, things, and habits with some effort. It takes time to squeeze dirty water from a sponge, but, with a little effort, you can make the space for something clean. Once your life is clear of anything or anyone causing undesirable outcomes, your true desires can fill the void. With a little effort, you can maintain your life's purpose for as long as you want.

One of the things I find business owners have a hard time removing is problem employees. When I first opened my practice, I had a hard time firing people, too. I remember one receptionist who I knew needed to be fired. My consultant at the time gave me a win-win concept to consider.

He asked me if this receptionist was serving my patients or enhancing the practice's purpose. Was maintaining the employment fair to my patients, my other staff members, and to me as well as her? I said no. He asked if I thought my practice was allowing the receptionist to live up to her true potential and if she was happy. I knew this wasn't the case because I had given her many chances to change her habits. Her attitude absolutely reflected her unhappiness.

He explained to me that I was causing her more harm than good. She obviously wasn't happy or living up to her potential. Keeping her on was counterproductive—for everyone. She needed a reason to seek out the career that was best for her and I was holding her back. In fact, I was enabling her to stay in a position or in a place where she was not happy.

Ever since then, I've had no trouble firing anyone. Who am I to stunt their potential?

The tree knows that if it holds onto its dead or dying leaves, it could cause harm to the tree itself. Often we ignore what needs to be let go because, at least immediately, it feels easier to be hurt than to hurt others. But how harmless is it really? You're letting others hurt you which might later cause them the very hurt you were looking to avoid. Or perhaps you only think you're protecting them from harm when, in reality, you're holding them back from success. This is the reward you give to yourself and others. It is the motivation for progress and healthful change.

Rewards are usually associated with your feelings. The feeling attached to a reward will determine the value you give it. Rewards can promote joy and happiness, but also sadness and depression. You may be rewarded with ten dollars, but you need a thousand dollars to pay your bills. You may feel sadness with that amount. Some people are motivated by pain and some are motivated by pleasure.

Having a lack in your life may cause you to feel fear, motivating you into action. You might attract pain into your life – perhaps a lack of money or a lack of love – so you can be motivated to pursue what's lacking. Or if you're motivated by pleasure you may pursue praise or require a constant showering of gifts as motivation. That behavior perpetuates a false sense of security.

Do you feel you deserve the rewards you desire? Do you attract people and things that continually cause you pain? Do you have characteristics that are not conducive to a healthy lifestyle? Do you cheat, lie, take advantage of, demean and hurt others mentally or physically? Do you love money and will you compromise on core principles to get it? Do you allow people to demean or take advantage of you?

Do you smoke, drink excessively, do drugs, overeat, or overspend? Do you hoard your money? Do you avoid love so as not to get hurt?

What types of situations do you enter into? For instance, do you always find yourself in debt, in agitating or abusive relationships? Are you constantly jumping from job to job?

The answers to all of these questions are the rewards you continually attract or avoid based on the feelings they stimulate.

The Rewards Exercise

Make a list of the rewards in your life and write next to each one the feelings attached to them. Write both "positive" and "negative" rewards.

For example, do you reward yourself with cigarettes when you are stressed out? What feeling is associated with cigarettes? Maybe you feel overwhelmed, scared, or worthless so you need to smoke?

Do you reward yourself with a salary that is too low to meet your needs? What feeling is attached to that? Do you feel good about it or do you feel anxiety?

Do you reward yourself with junk food and sugary drinks? Do you feel secure or relaxed when you eat them or angry with yourself?

Did you reward yourself with a mutually loving relationship or marriage?

After writing out your rewards, review the ones that bring an imbalance to your life. Are you able to detach from them? What would you need to do to change them? What support from others would you need? Review the list and determine which reward is stopping you from receiving other rewards.

Let's look at this example: if you reward yourself with alcohol or drugs, how will you be able to detach from this? Do you need to avoid your drinking buddies or the people supplying you with drugs? Who in your life can support you in that decision? How is this behavior stopping you from receiving other rewards? Maybe these rewards are affecting your sales. Maybe clients smell alcohol on your breath or you're too high to focus and work effectively.

Maybe your current salary isn't enough for you and you want to make more.

Write your answers under the new heading of "Rewards" on your Autumn List.

RELATIONSHIPS

The last 'R' stands for Relationships which can range from very loose to very tight connections or attachments to people, things, and events in your business and life.

You will be evaluating the relationships you have formed and whether they are still advantageous to your business and life. These are your connections to the outside world as well as the relationship you have developed with your self.

The tree in autumn is cutting off its relationship to the outside world and is focusing its efforts on conserving energy. It takes a lot of energy to grow and keep leaves and fruit.

Your autumn is the time for you to determine if the relationships you have are worth the energy you expend on them. It truly does take energy to keep and maintain any relationship. Especially when the person, thing, or event takes without giving. You might make the decision to what I call "autumnize," or eliminate this relationship or connection for your own benefit.

Come to think of it, are you a drain on someone else? Are you a damaged leaf that someone else needs to autumnize? Instead of being terminated, maybe you've been autumnized. By not separating yourself from them, you do neither yourself nor them any favors by anchoring to someone or something that is no longer beneficial. You aren't giving yourself the opportunity to pursue better options.

Relationships can take the guise of your place of business, your home or neighborhood, or the drama in your business and life. Examples can be going to board meetings you now hate to attend, family outings that cause you anxiety, or your marriage to your spouse, business and other entities.

Autumn and its counterpart, spring, are the transformational seasons. This is where change occurs. Any change that occurs in a given structure is caused by disconnected and reattached atoms and the transference of energy.

But why is it so much easier for the tree to change than us? The tree prunes itself without needing to understand how everything will benefit from its actions. It simply does it and the benefits happen automatically. Nature also prunes the tree through storms. I don't think it complains but innately knows this is a benefit not only for itself, but for all those who interact with it.

We are hesitant to prune our lives, maintaining the illusion that it is more painful to change than to continue with a bad system. We assume the benefits of that change will never come. But that's only true as long as nothing changes. If no energy is transferred from poor habits to good ones -- if the disconnection never occurs -- then what you reap will always be what you've sown. Re-planting a dead tree is pointless.

Your problems or challenges are your storms whereby the seasons are forcing you to prune. Innately you know this as well but resistance is part of human nature.

Pain and pleasure are very powerful motivators. The exercise below shows you how to evaluate your relationships ahead of time, recognize when pain is coming, and make the decision to kill the monster in its crib.

You may feel like you're hurting people by disconnecting from them. But remember, a bad relationship can be a detriment to everyone involved. If you don't do it, it's inevitable that something will happen that is out of your control to make that change if the universe feels there's an imbalance. It's always best, in situations where the quality of a relationship is called into question, to stay in the driver's seat. The changes you make should follow your desires.

If you're distraught at having so little money to run your business or you seem to have continual staff problems, it is certainly less painful to keep the status quo than to invoke and actualize your season of autumn to start the change. But autumn will come. It may come tomorrow, next month, or a year from now, but something will break if the situation is out of balance. We've all heard it before, but rarely do we ever personally put it into action: Life is all about balance. Change happens with or without us. Inaction just overcorrects the scales, which is an imbalance in itself.

That burning desire for change, left unattended, causes arguments. Each party's desperate need to disconnect from the pain will boil over. Fighting occurs when we're caught up in wanting the other to fill their void instead of learning from each other how to strengthen our weakest traits. When another person doesn't fill their void in the way they want it filled, whether through attack or retreat, they will protect themselves.

In a fight, you are protecting yourself. Many people want to have an argument with someone so they can have an excuse to release that person from their life instead of making the conscious decision to do so before it has a chance to happen.

The Relationship Exercise

Write the last header – 'Relationships' – on your Autumn List and think about the following questions:

What is the quality of your relationships? What types of people are involved in your business and life and what kinds of relationship do you have with them? You may have a boss, but is this person supportive or domineering? Do you have staff who don't listen to you or refuse to work as a team? Are your friends leeching off you because of who you are or how much money you make? Are your friends supporting you in habits that are not conducive to a healthy lifestyle? Do you have a partner or spouse who puts you down to maintain a feeling of superiority? Do you have the relationship you want with your children?

Who and/or what is stopping you from connecting to quality relationships in your life? Is there someone in your family or company who overspends?

Do you have addictions? Are you a workaholic, an alcoholic, or drug addict? Do you have unhealthy eating habits, smoke cigarettes, or do anything else enabling addiction or an inability to autumnize a habit?

Do you have love or friendship in your life? Do you have certain characteristics or qualities that cause people to avoid you? Do you have people in your life who give you false hope or love?

This exercise is essential for understanding the connections that are no longer beneficial. Have you gone through a breakup, a divorce, or has a loved one or pet passed away? Holding onto a past relationship keeps you living in an irreversible past, missing out on your present, and denying your future.

Are you losing your business or high performing employees because of someone in your office? Have you been through a tragedy and are now taking out your anger on employees, family, or customers?

If a loved one has passed, one of the best ways to get through this difficult time is to recognize the beneficial relationships you already have with family and friends or even a support group. No one need forget a loved one's passing, but with time you can learn to use what you've learned from the experience to enhance and enrich your life. I strongly believe that people come into our lives for specific reasons, whether for short or long periods of time. To avoid using that experience as a means of growth would be, in my opinion, a disrespectful waste of that relationship.

This is the process of detaching.

If you're unable to detach from relationships causing you a detriment, holding onto them can stop you from developing new relationships that might change your business or allow you to go on living. How can a new leaf grow while the old one is still there?

Write down every relationship you presently have in your life. Examine the quality of that relationship using a scale of 1 – 5 in which 5 is excellent. What feeling is attached to that relationship? Write down the number and feeling next to each relationship you've listed. Now repeat that exercise using any recent relationship that is no longer in your life. This will help you see how each relationship brings a lesson or a benefit. Now, note which ones still feel "active."

Ask yourself who and/or what is stopping you from improving or detaching from all of the relationships you've now listed? How can each relationship be improved or released?

Don't forget to look at your actions as well. Notice when you're maintaining or creating false relationships. A false relationship is a connection with someone who is more concerned about what he or she can get from you than reciprocity.

Most importantly, look at your relationship with yourself. This can be most difficult because it is easier to blame others instead of taking responsibility for your past decisions and actions or non-actions.

AUTUMNIZE

So how did it all go? You were probably amazed by what feelings you attached to the roles, rewards, and relationships in your life. Many of you may be having a hard time deciding to detach and that's okay. These people, things, and events may have been in your life for such a long time that until now, you never realized how detrimental they've been.

However, I want you to realize that these relationships were beneficial for you at that time. That's why they were in your life. Now you can see they no longer serve you and new relationships need to be formed or old ones renegotiated.

There are countless stories of people being fired who are now doing what they really love. That's the benefit of autumnizing or being autumnized. It's all in how you perceive the disconnection.

What happens when a leaf detaches from a tree? It's leaving what it knows best. It was born there. It's familiar. But when it is released, it becomes alone in flight. The world that it knows swiftly changes.

The leaf can try to hold on to the branch, but will still die because of the lack of nutrients from the tree. It will still be alone, since all the other leaves have left.

Or it can land by the base of the tree. Then, at least it's near what it knows.

Or it can accept the detachment and trust that the wind will take it to where it belongs. Maybe it's needed by the base of the tree or maybe it's needed somewhere far away.

The good part about being human as opposed to a leaf is that we're conscious of this process. These are our choices.

We can be scared of being alone, not allowing ourselves to detach from the very thing or person that cannot support us. Staying is still loneliness, but we justify it to ourselves because at least we're familiar with our surroundings.

We can finally detach, but fight all the things that come into our lives, still holding close to what we know, refusing to use new strategies to get to where we really need to be because we refuse to let go of where we think we need to be. We may make decisions that keep us in the state of lacking. The lack of money, the lack of close and loyal friends, the lack of someone supportive. Landing in the area where we are unable to affect change or growth.

The leaf that falls to the earth is broken down into its basic components during autumn so it can be used again in another way.

The same is true with your autumn. Once you fully detach and fill that void with something beneficial, you will attract the people and things necessary for rebirth and grow into the person you want to be.

Perhaps it's not even so drastic as total detachment. You may just need to re-evaluate an old relationship with new strategies.

When I experienced the closing of my 15-year-old practice due to a disability, the death of my mom and dad, the ending of my marriage, and so many other things, I didn't realize that I'd never made time to really mourn those losses. I really didn't want to address my emotions or re-evaluate these relationships, but understood that if I didn't, I wouldn't be able to grow and evolve into the person I knew I needed to become. Initially, it was not a pretty sight.

But after a while, peace came over me. I came to realize that, even though I was alone and there were voids there for the first time, I needed to become more aware. Aware that God, The Universe, Source, my inner being, or whatever you want to call it, was going to bring me what I really needed, only if I allowed it to happen and if I accepted it. If I just had the innocent trust of a leaf on the breeze.

Don't fight it. Don't resist it, even on the whitewater. Let the river of life take you to a wide and abundant sea.

AUTUMN EXERCISES (Hard Assessment)

BUSINESS QUESTIONS:

a. Am I willing to dissect my business and remove what is no longer working?

b. What or who in my business needs to be Autumnized (Removed or changed)? And, am I willing to remove any employees or customers who are a negative impact on the business?

c. Am I willing to analyze my products or services and change or remove the ones that are no longer impacting the business in a positive way?

d. Am I a micromanager in the business? Unable to detach from daily operations?

e. Am I willing to fire myself from certain functions?

f. Do I need to limit TV, video games and such that may stop me from creating a webinar, creating and perfecting my pitch, improve my marketing or closing skills, and things like that which will increase my profits? Do I need help doing this?

PERSONAL QUESTIONS:

a. What relationships are no longer working in my life that need to be removed or perhaps, analyzed further?

b. Do I need to temporarily separate for a while to reevaluate later?

c. Do I need to eliminate or decrease the number of hours certain roles in my life are no longer working well for me?

d. Do I need to eliminate certain addictions such as cigarettes, drugs, unhealthy foods and drinks, etc.

e. Do I need to limit TV, video games and such that may stop me from furthering my education, reading or other habits that will enhance my life?

CHAPTER ELEVEN

WINTER - BE STILL AND NOTICE THE POWER

Winter may seem useless to some. It's cold, few things are living, and it causes nothing but heartache to the animals that need shelter. Besides skiing or snowboarding or riding on snowmobiles, what good is it for?

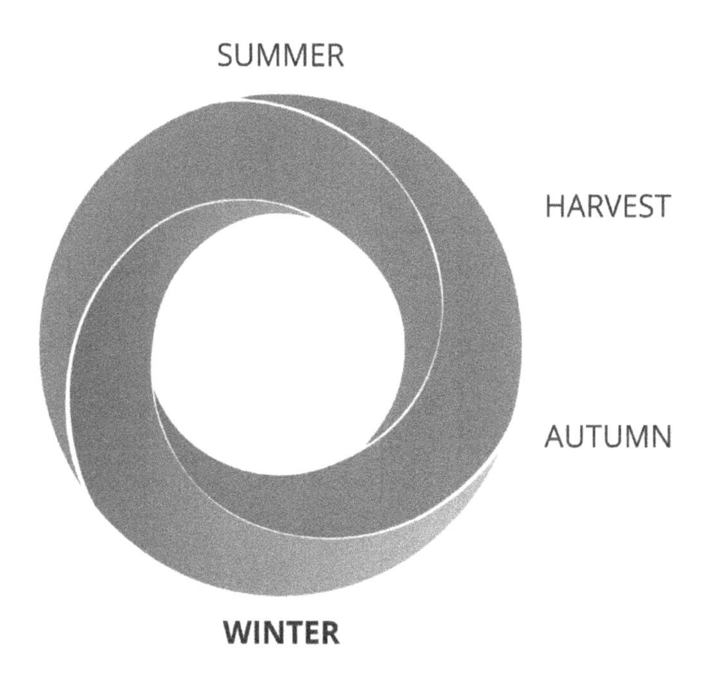

Winter is stillness, the recouping stage of life. It is the season for storing your potential power. In summer, the leaves create a barrier blocking a view of the inner forest. But in winter the view within is clear.

When detaching from harmful people and things in autumn, you give yourself a break from continual irritation so any wounds can be healed. Winter gives you the opportunity to tap into your vulnerability so you can more clearly see what needs to be healed and to abandon what no longer works. This is why the season is one of dormancy and hibernation, or even barrenness and sterility depending on the situation.

Once your strength is restored in winter, you will be able to relinquish the power within and move into the next season. Winter allows us to go within and realize the potential power that lies beneath our illusions.

Winter is the time to be still and plan, to quiet the mind so that we can listen to our inner voice. It's difficult to properly plan when distracted by chores, conversation, and the chaos of life.

This is when you strategize. Without a plan, you may get to where you want to go, but the likelihood of it happening is slim. As they say, the person with a broken watch is right about the time twice a day.

Find a quiet place and think-listen-plan. Look back at your past summer, the fruits of your labor. You went through harvest and autumn to make the barren visible. Envelop yourself in the solace of that calm.

Keeping a journal, meditating, or sleeping allows you to re-sequence past events, decisions, and desires. Through these techniques, you can determine how they can be put to use. From there, you can prepare them to be united in your purpose to create and grow powerful new desires.

If you were to bypass winter, you would never learn from your past decisions and would continue to manifest lacking and misery. This season is a time to reflect on the knowledge already within yourself and to store the most useful knowledge you've gained from others.

By accepting your desire to replenish (harvest) and cultivating a willingness to detach from people, things, and events that are no longer working (autumn), you can then use winter to tap into knowledge and understanding. From there, your desired direction and purpose can be seeded.

Meditate on your autumnization process. Winter is your realization. You may not need to detach from that person, job, or situation, but simply release the old relationship to form a new one. Create a new contract so that the relationship can work better.

Let's say one of your best employees quits. You start looking for another person, but, in the meantime, you need your other employees to pick up the slack. Days and weeks go by and that employee isn't replaced. Your other employees are working hard to maintain productivity. You realize that the work is getting done and you are saving a ton of money! So, you let it go.

The breaking point is when resentment starts to build among your staff. You never sat in the contemplation of winter and examined the possible downsides and upsides to your decision. Maybe there is someone already on your staff who could be promoted to the empty position. Perhaps you need to renegotiate the contract you have with your employees. Or maybe what you see as efficiency is overworking a particular group of people in the company and the distribution of tasks needs to be re-evaluated.

But without reflection, that employee quitting leaves a gap in your plan for efficiency. The extra work placed on others may not be that much, but without compensating them for those tasks or renegotiating their duties, you have a potentially damaging problem. Take time to look for the gift within the circumstances. From there the solutions directing your desires can emerge.

Taking the time for reflection, tapping into your own wisdom, talking to key members of your staff, or asking for help from outside of your business can help you to formulate an effective plan of management. Ignoring the issue, reacting negatively, or just going into a protective mode could cause your business to lose even more staff in the process and eventually customers.

The true purpose of winter is to seek out the truth. It is your decision and yours alone to take your past suffering and turn it into a benefit. The truth in winter is the benefit and knowledge gained through that decision. Avoid the falsehoods and illusions of the outside world telling you that nothing can be learned through strife. The truth in winter is gleaned from your perception and interpretation.

Winter guides you to determine if you need to change your direction or reorganize your priorities for what you want to manifest. You take what you learned in autumn and create a plan for better and more abundant fruit next summer.

When I first completed this exercise for myself, I looked at both my goal list for the year prior and my Autumn List. I realized I wasn't achieving certain goals because of the road blocks I had on my Autumn List. Until I rid myself of the people and things on that list, certain goals would not come to fruition.

I created a plan for actualizing my Autumn List and, as the process of letting go started, my perception of my self-worth increased.

There were some interesting things on that list. Some were the results of decisions I'd made long ago. I wondered to myself, "What the heck was I thinking?" But it quickly became clear that I needed to make these decisions so that I could release certain characteristics within me of which I wasn't previously aware. I wasn't aware of them precisely because I didn't want to see them. If I had seen them, I would have realized just how they were screwing up my life and I'd have to do something about them.

In autumn, you made a list of what you needed to detach from your life. In winter, you will take that list and determine exactly what you won't allow to be a drain on your energy any longer.

1. Look at your Autumn List and pick no more than two things you listed under each of the Three R's. These are your starting points. Try your best to pick the most important or effectual attachments. Instead of pruning each individual leaf, your goal should be to prune the branch. Search for that connection. What you'll notice is that by detaching one thing on your list, others will follow.

2. Once you determine this, ask yourself the following questions:

a. "Why did I attract this into my life at that time?"

b. "What did it try to teach me?"

c. "Did I learn from it?"

d. "If not, how can I learn from it?"

e. "If I did learn from it, do I no longer need this in my life or can I continue to learn from it?"

3. Answer all of the above for each of those things chosen from your lists under the Three R's.

4. Once you have performed this exercise, place the items on another sheet of paper for the next exercise.

Remember, this is an exercise of awareness. Your goal is to seek out what needs to be detached and no longer allowed to remain in your life or business.

This isn't meant to overwhelm you. Take your time. If you can't find the time to do the entire exercise, then do parts of it as you can. The important thing to remember is to just do something. Even if you desperately want someone or something out of your life, don't be surprised that you may resist the process. When you've been working against yourself for so long, it's natural to feel uncomfortable feeling comfortable.

You may feel like you're mourning the death of a part of you. But that's because this is exactly what you're going through. It's winter. You may feel alone, scared, or unwilling to do what you know needs to be done. You may feel a fear of the unknown. But what is death? It's a result of the detachment from one form into another that creates a transformation and a transition. It will be used to fertilize the soil for growth, as will that leaf that lies on the ground awaiting a new purpose.

WINTER EXERCISES (Planning)

BUSINESS QUESTIONS:

1. What is my plan to reorganize and regulate my business?

a. Am I willing to take the time to create an effective plan of action?

b. What is my new vision of my business and what are the key objectives for achieving the results I want? What are the results I am looking for in my new summer?

c. What strategies do I need to implement my plan?

d. Do I have determined milestones (schedules and goals), tasks and responsibilities for plan execution?

e. What systems need to be revamped or replaced to ensure the plans our executed effectively?

f. Is my system of communication, whether internally and externally, in place to receive feedback from my employees, customers, vendors, and suppliers?

g. Can I build a plan myself that addresses what I learned in prior seasons or do I need outside help? Do I have the skills and staff to execute on any plans I put together? If not, what or who do I need?

h. What experts do I have in my network that can give me the knowledge to create the plans I need to enhance the effectiveness of my vision I have for my business?

i. Are we properly staffed to meet the milestones, tasks and responsibilities we are setting? Are their weaknesses in the organization, especially in functional management that can limit success? How can we correct them?

2. Am I protecting my business from outside forces?

a. Do I have enough insurance coverage?

b. Do I have written policies that protect the business from customer and employee lawsuits? Is my behavior and the behavior of my employees protecting the reputation of the business?

c. Do I have ironclad contracts with customers and employees so there is no confusion of what is expected of me and what is expected of them? Do I have a proper partnership agreement?

d. Do I have a team of professionals ready for any circumstances that I cannot handle by myself?

PERSONAL QUESTIONS

a. How do I envision my relationships, marriage, family, etc.?

b. Am I unorganized and have clutter all around me?

c. Do I not finish my tasks no matter how close I come to completing them?

d. Do I need outside help to receive the knowledge that I need to move forward? Do I need a mentor, coach, therapist, health practitioner, etc.?

e. Am I willing to decrease the chaos in my life and become quieter?

f. Am I willing to focus on my life and follow through on my plan?

CHAPTER TWELVE

RELINQUIS – TIME TO SHOW THEM WHAT YOU'VE GOT

Napoleon Hill, author of *Think and Grow Rich,* mentions desire as one of the principles for success. But not half-hearted desire as in, I would like to have success, or It would be nice to have success, or I really desire success but I need to do some other things first before I look at what I want. Hill calls it a "burning" desire, as if you'd rather die than miss out on achieving your goals. Why burning? Because when something is heated, the atoms release energy in the form of an explosive reaction.

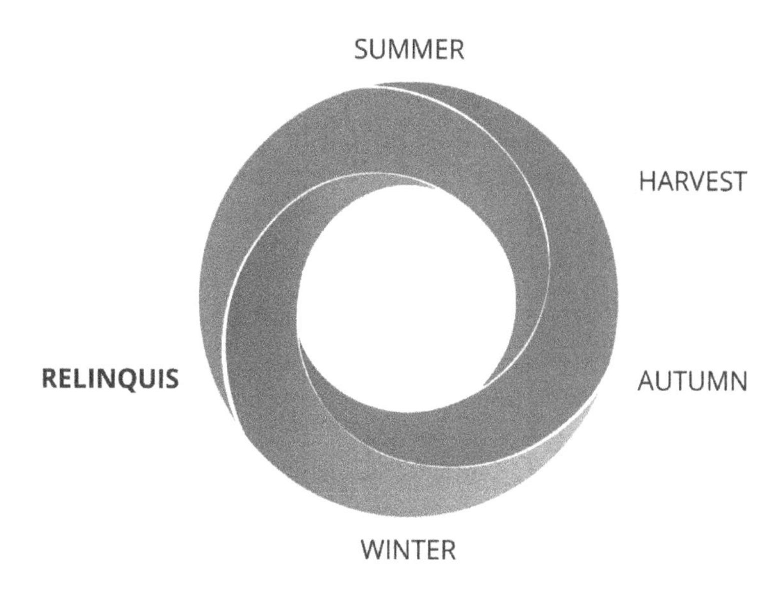

The season of "burning" desire is relinquis. In winter, potential power is held in storage—usually frozen. Heat melts winter's barrier. Reflecting upon and tapping into your power in winter is the first step. To remove any barriers, you need to turn up the heat of your desire for change.

Let's return to our example of the tree. Winter has afforded it rest, it has stored its energy, and it is now ready to continue with its cyclical purpose in relinquis. The tree's branches begin budding and drawing in the soil's nutrients for growth. It's preparing for the connection it needs to perpetuate itself in spring. It has sequenced its atoms in winter in such a way as to make itself attractive.

This season is nature's internal execution. It has a plan and now, before anything happens on the outside, the inside needs to start turning its wheels to implement it.

The plant starts its inner workings to open the flower and expel it fragrance, secrete its nectar or release its pollen Without the internal execution, its true essence will never be realized by the outside world.

Relinquis is the law of attraction. This law is only one sixth of your success process, but it's just as vital as the rest. If you don't prepare in winter for the realization of your desire in relinquis, your attractiveness to others and what they may offer to the success of your business or life will be effectually limited.

If you don't create an appealing logo, slogan, product or anything else to supply to your customer, they will go to your competition every time. Something is always needed as a lure. In nature, this is why the peacock displays bright colors, the nightingale sings such a sweet song, and the sunflower is so large and ostentatious.

Can your product compete with these examples or does it need some work?

Relinquis is also the surrendering season. If the ice never surrenders the powerful water within, then nothing will grow.

If the flower never surrenders its nectar or the bird its song, nothing can regenerate.

In relinquis you release the power within, sending a signal to all to come and enjoy your product, whether you're selling a service, a book, or even yourself.

This is also the season in which you forgive and are grateful. To forgive is to forgo what is within you. If you do not forgive, you hold on to negative feelings. By forgiving, you open up as the flower does. If the flower does not do this, it will starve and perish. You will too because nothing can be given or received due to your wall of protection.

Relinquis opens in order for growth to occur and if you are not forgiving, then you will not fully grow and feel incomplete.

As I said earlier, people and things in your life can be viewed as holding you back or compelling you to realize opportunities. It depends on what side of the coin you see.

Gratitude and forgiveness are synonymous. They are both actions of relinquis. They release the feelings associated with the items on your Autumn List. Many of you have deeply rooted feelings attached to these items. Being grateful for the experience of having had what is no longer working in your life, and thereby forgiving any indiscretions, sends an important and empowering message that they were there to help you grow. When you believe that, you can begin to build your reality apart from their influence. Ingratitude simply reinforces the illusion that you have no control. Or, even worse, that you're unworthy of control.

Believing your worthiness opens the flood gates to getting what you want—that attractive desire.

I've had patients say, "I cannot be grateful for what may be coming. My record is one of lifelong failure and disease."

With this type of thinking, I have them perceive it in a different way. I tell them not to be grateful for what has yet to physically manifest, but to be grateful for the desire to have it. Desire fuels manifestation.

> Believing your worthiness opens the floodgates to getting what you want – that attractive desire.

By focusing your gratitude on the desire, you change your energy. This energy transforms what and how you attract.

You want that big account? You want to increase your salary or commission? You want a deeper love with your spouse? Then the first step to achieving your goal is to be grateful for the desire to change and for the foundation it affords your future manifestations.

If your business was on the verge of bankruptcy and then you won $10 million, how would your energy change? Before the money even made it to your bank account, before you ever even saw a single cent, you'd be grateful and eager for the opportunity coming your way.

This is what people mean when they say, "Fake it 'til you make it!"

You are fueling the desire within which will cause you to create the growth available in spring. The pollination of flowers depends on how sweet they look and actually taste. Likewise, the growth of your business is dependent on communication with your potential customer and then on your ability to deliver on promises.

To reiterate: one of things that will hold you back from fully experiencing relinquis is being unable to forgive. But with proper gratitude, forgiveness (of yourself or others) becomes unnecessary. If you're grateful for the desire to affect change in the future, then you've found the hidden benefit. You've found the gift.

It's important for me to be very clear here. I understand that some of you may have gone through terrible experiences in the past. No one can diminish the effects of that. I can only offer a perspective for future growth and reiterate that I've seen my method work with countless patients and how nature really works.

There's an old saying I tell my patients: "Holding onto anger is like drinking poison and hoping the other person dies." Unless others decide to be affected, anger or any emotion stopping you from moving forward only affects you.

Your past decisions created and filled your voids to point you toward finding your purpose. By being grateful, you automatically forgive those past decisions and come to understand their deeper purpose. The people and things involved in those decisions will also be automatically forgiven. If it weren't for them, you would never have had those experiences which caused you to decide to change your life.

Your trials and tribulations are your gifts—the potential power within you waiting to be released.

Take a look at your winter exercise and, out of the three choices, pick the one that you have the most desire to accomplish.

For example, a patient of mine realized she was always micromanaging her staff. She was so involved with micromanagement that she didn't have any time to network, which she enjoyed and at which she excelled.

On her list, she had : *Stop micromanaging and hire a manager* (*Roles*), *Create a 10-week course* (*Rewards*), *and Go out and network to sell the new 10-week course* (*Relationships*).

She couldn't abandon her duties as the owner/manager and start working on the program, or just walk out and start networking. Her first step was to find and train a manager.

She'd then be free to create her course. From there, her consulting business grew exponentially. Her desire and enthusiasm to create a course was so attractive that people were quickly signing up.

The stress of micromanaging everyone stopped her from doing what she wanted to do. She was afraid of handing over the management position to anyone else and trusting they'd do a good job. Once she let go of that fear and tapped into the energy of her burning desire, nothing further stood in the way of her success.

The Gratitude List:

People often ask me if I had to pick one thing that could start a change in their business or life, what would that be? I tell them about the Gratitude List.

Gratitude melts the barrier of negativity and allows the true self to appear. This is what causes people and events to be attracted to you. No more barrier of fear, resentment, or protection. Just pure energy ready to be transformed into whatever you desire.

(*Go to my website at www.dragrios.com/gratitudelist for a free video that explains this more in depth but with a twist.*)

Follow these steps to create your Gratitude List:

a. Write down all the people, things, and events since birth that you're grateful for—the good and the bad, especially the most difficult times in your life. Often, they're your best teachers.

b. Remember to include you. You're here and have the potential to accomplish your desires. Be grateful for that potential.

c. Read your list out loud in the morning and before bed. You can even read it to yourself at work as a reminder. This will help you to focus your sense of gratitude.

d. If you're having trouble noticing the benefit of being wronged or in your own previously hurtful mistakes, follow these steps:

i. Realize that this process can take some time and give yourself a break. Don't put so much pressure on feeling better immediately.

ii. Find a therapist, coach, spiritual teacher or whomever you feel will be able to help you. You don't have to do this alone.

iii. Remind yourself that people do the best they can with the resources available.

iv. Realize that the previous line applies to you, too. Don't overextend your resources out of impatience.

One of the most important things I've learned from all of my experiences is that without finding the gift within everyone and everything, you'll keep going through the seasons until you do. I can't tell you how many times I had to go on that ride. You can learn from my past decisions or make your own. Some people need to reinvent the wheel instead of adding more bling to it.

Everyone does the best they can with the resources they have. Everything in my life, whether it was being hurt or hurting someone else, led me to the discovery of *Life's One Law*. I chose to take all of it, lay it all out on the table and use it to guide myself and many others.

RELINQUIS EXERCISE (Internal Execution)

BUSINESS QUESTIONS:

a. Am I willing to reveal my new vision/plan to my employees and/or customers? If not, why not? Am I not ready or I am a perfectionist and feel it is not ready for review?

b. How is my new plan and strategies going to impact our new culture, the business, our customers, etc.?

c. Are my employees passionate about my new vision and plan to serve our customers and community and their roles in it?

d. If not, how am I going to translate my passion and the new culture to my employees so they can feel the same?

e. How will we communicate and implement our new passion and culture regarding our customers, vendors and suppliers?

f. Are we getting involved and/or serving the needs of the community, other businesses and individuals? How are we giving?

g. Do my customers feel valued by me and my employees? Are we giving more value than what they paid for?

h. Do I give too much to my customers? Do I let them take advantage of me? Am I valuing my time?

PERSONAL QUESTIONS:

a. Do I value myself and not allow others to take advantage of my kindness and servitude? Do others feel that I value them?

b. Am I serving others in a way that is of worth to them?

c. Am I giving money, my time or something else to my community or the less fortunate?

d. Do I love others in a way that I would want to be loved?

e. Do I allow other to take advantage of my kindness?

CHAPTER THIRTEEN

SPRING – CREATE A RAPPORT

Spring, the season of connection, is when relationships are made and flourish. During this season, you communicate with your outside world that attracts those pollinators. This linking causes things to happen in this time of year so that you can have a fruitful summer.

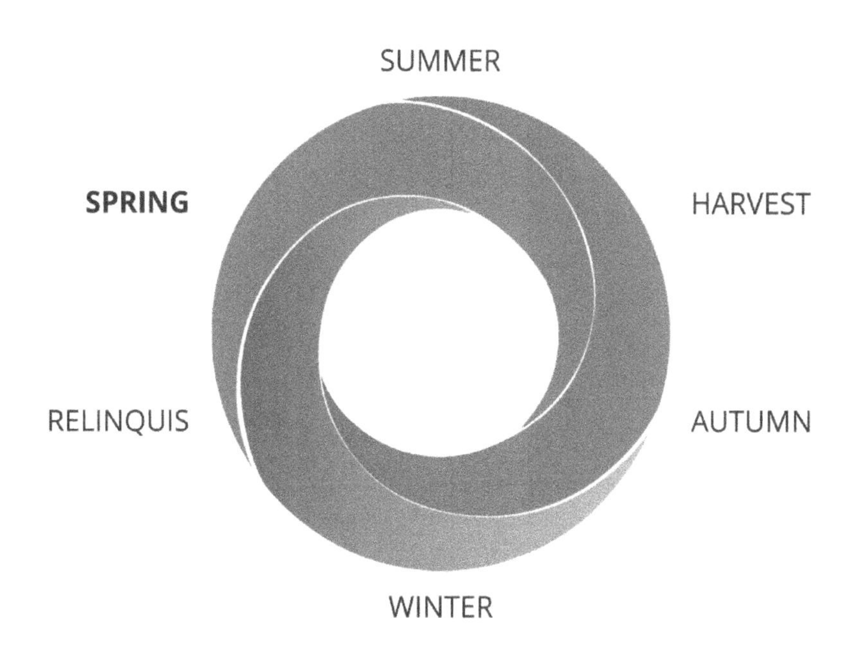

April showers bring May flowers. The life-giving water needs to connect to foliage that is so thirsty for its molecules to trigger a rebirth. Bonding with the right type of client is your opportunity to breathe new life into your business or keep your growth continuing.

If you are not open to new connections or reconnecting to old ones, then you risk the chance of stifling your growth, whether in business or in any of life's relationships.

In relinquis, nature is being supplied. Rain is falling, ice is melting and flowers are starting to bloom. This season is the emergence of what has been dormant in winter. In business, this is the phase when you are ready to send out a signal, you are ready to connect. This is what happens at the beginning of a networking function. Everyone is showing what they have and trying to meet others.

But no deal can be made until a connection is formed. This is spring.

Spring is the season when pollinators seek to fertilize. You are in business to sell and to be sold something. You need things to run your business. Actually, everything you do or accept is due to you or someone selling. You sold your spouse to marry you. You were sold on having kids. The list is endless. That's why, as the adage goes, nothing happens until somebody sells something. Communication is essential to selling and the better your communication, the more you will sell.

This is why winter is necessary for spring to happen. If you make a clear plan in winter of what you want your summer to look like, then you will know exactly what pollinators you need and how to attract them.

In relinquis, you prepared yourself to become appealing to those pollinators and now spring is here so you can encourage them to choose you and not your competition.

If you were a sunflower looking for pollinators such as bees to connect with but you had no nectar, the bees would move on to the next sunflower. Simple as that.

Relinquis prepares you for spring. It releases to the outside world your inner supply and then spring makes a connection so a rapport is created. You create more long-term relationships with a rapport than by merely an association. The length of that relationship will be determined by the strength of the bond.

Relinquis is the attraction season and the one who has the most supply wins. It's imperative to make sure your relinquis has positioned you to attract as many customers as possible. Allow your desire, or your passion for what you do, to be released so people will want to work with you.

But, if you only look for bees, you'll miss out on other pollinators who may also fertilize your business. Major chains have gone out of business because they relied on one pollinator or one concept. They didn't understand the environment changed and did not adapt to it. The tree or any species dies only when they are unable or unwilling to adapt to the changes of the ecosystem.

It's a mistake many business owners make when they go to networking meetings. They only look for the businesses that they think are their main pollinators, missing out on business owners who may bring something new to the table or know the pollinator they seek.

Paying attention is how the top sales and business performers make it to the top. They diversify who they're meeting to include both ingenuity and expertise, opening themselves up (relinquis) to any potential pollinators (spring) who can close the sale.

If you're accustomed to doing business with birds, that's no reason to ignore the bees. If you're clear and know precisely what you're looking for, then go for it. You may have a niche and know who is your best pollinator. But always include flexibility in your plan. When generals put a plan into action, the plan shifts as the enemy's response demands.

Spring is the builder. How do you build something? You need to connect or link objects together. This is the season of building relationships. If you can't approach and start talking to other business owners at that networking meeting, then you will limit your new business opportunities. The sunflower isn't a dull color. It's bright with a huge black bull's-eye. This is how it communicates to its pollinators. Don't be afraid to show your colors.

If you are not an effective communicator, then take courses or hire someone who will help you with this. This is essential to build a community of customers or clients. Commune is the base word of communication. It is to build rapport.

But remember, relinquis and spring are when plants, trees and flowers are budding and being fertilized. You aren't going to get summer immediately. I've had patients come to me upset because they weren't seeing results as quickly as they anticipated—whether with their health or business. But, all things in time. Be grateful for the budding and the slowly mounting fertility. Summer will be here before you know it.

You may be going to networking meetings and failing to land many deals because no rapport was created. You may get very upset. But, without you even being aware of it, there's budding happening. Sometimes rapport can be built immediately; sometimes it takes time to build.

You're putting yourself out there, which automatically increases your chances of closing a deal. Don't stop going but look at your effectiveness in expressing what you want.

Try changing your pitch. Maybe you are overly communicating and overwhelming your audience, causing them to be confused and not allowing a rapport to be created. Practice in front of the mirror or in front of someone who will give you honest feedback.

Soon you'll have a meeting. Then, it's important to recognize where the deal is in its maturation. If the deal hasn't matured yet and you're pushing for spring while you're still in relinquis, you risk it falling through. You can never pick the apple before it's ripe or if it hasn't emerged yet. Recognizing where the deal is in its progression will decrease your stress and anticipation. How many times did you force a deal which fell through because you didn't allow things to sequence properly?

The calmer you are and the more you simply allow the season to do what it does best, the better your results. You need to make sure – before you move to the next season – that you've done all you can to fulfill the current season's purpose. Notice whether or not it's served you to the best of its ability. If it has, push ahead, but never before.

At times you may be uncertain what season you are in because of the transition period between each. Focus on the previous season and make sure you've done everything you possibly could before moving on.

Remember, spring is all about building rapport. Here are some ways you can improve this.

SPRING EXERCISE (External Execution)

BUSINESS QUESTIONS:

My Implementation

a. I have good rapport with my employees, customers and anyone else I meet? Am I over negotiating with vendors and suppliers by grinding them down and forgetting they are running a business as well?

b. How well do I communicate my vision and new plan to employees, customers and community? Is it too much and not clear and concise?

c. Do I need to improve my communication skills? What books or programs can I buy or what experts can I hire to improve or get past a fear I might have? Am I willing to practice my new skills?

d. If I am not willing to do that, then who can I hire to communicate my passion and vision?

Business and Employee Implementation

a. Are we ready to act upon the return phone calls, emails and such when potential and existing clients connect with us?

b. How effective is our marketing plan and what will we do to ensure we follow it? Is our message clear and do we fully believe in our product or service?

c. On the sales front, are we communicating our value and closing deals?

d. Are we operating efficiently, delivering product as promised and on-time and supporting customers by "going the extra mile?"

e. Do we have open communications with employees, customers, suppliers and vendors so reporting is effective and does not get lost in the translation?

f. Do my employees have good rapport with themselves, customers, vendors and suppliers so that our operations run smoothly?

g. Are employees engaged in the day to day operations and care about the outcomes and goals they and the business has set for them?

PERSONAL QUESTIONS:

a. How well do I communicate with my loved ones, relatives and friends? Do I overtake the conversation or do I sit and engage very little?

b. Do I work on my personal relationships as I would with my customers or peers, or do I take them for granted and expect them to evolve without any effort or very little effort on my end?

c. Do you tell my family how it is regardless of their feelings? Do I use them as a pin cushion instead of a sound board? Try treating your family members, especially your kids as if they were the boss or customer. Not as if they are in charge of you but communicating to them with respect and love. The latter gives you a possible consequence, getting fired or losing a customer. Start respecting and communicating to them the way you do with your boss or customer and you will have less stress and dissidence.

d. You may be overcommunicative, actually talking yourself out of the deal. You may give too much information or overwhelm your prospective client. Listening after providing a concise pitch is invaluable. It will tell you how you'll need to shift your plans to meet their needs. Don't assume you know exactly what they need. They'll be happy to tell you. Listen carefully and then offer your solution.

e. If you feel you need to improve your personal and business communication skills, there are plenty of books and tutorials available. Hire coaches to get you past your fear. And then practice, practice, practice!

CHAPTER FOURTEEN

SUMMER - ARE YOU HAPPY WITH YOUR END RESULT?

Summer has finally arrived. You can now enjoy the fruit of your labor.

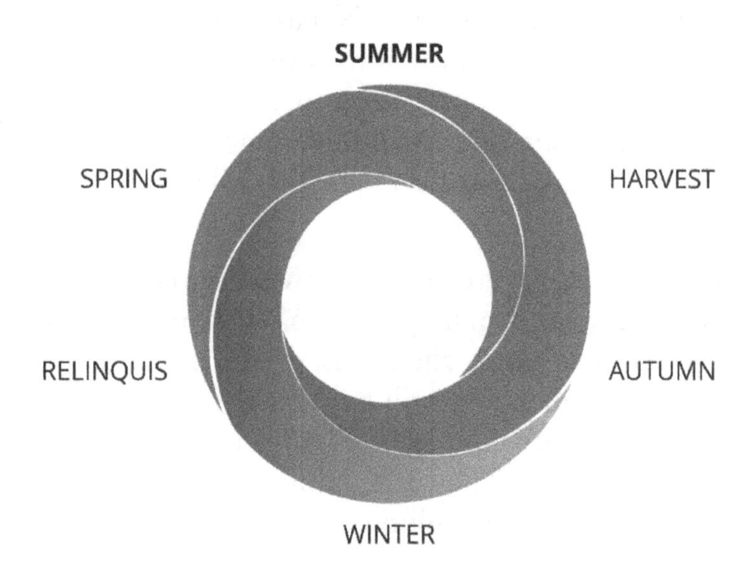

We've come full-circle and so we can compare the difference between this summer and the last. Remember, summer is decision time on the results you have created.

Was it what you expected? Did it need to be tweaked a bit? Or even overhauled? Don't worry if it didn't turn out exactly as you wanted this time around. The seasons are always happening and, with patience and preparation, you'll have chance after chance to achieve your goals.

Going through the seasons a second time should not be time consuming. Many times, a season or two just need to be tweaked. However, there are times where a season would need to be revamped.

Not only are you making decisions in this season, so is your client. After you connected in spring and communicated your offer with the benefits of your product or service, they need to decide whether to buy from you.

If they did, then you go into the next season of harvest and get paid. It's time to gather your well-deserved compensation for all of your hard work.

Even if your produce in summer is perfect, that doesn't mean you should leave the next production to chance. Each season is used – is put into action – to make sure the product gets better and better or keep with the times with each need for and desire to change.

The tree never says, "I feel like I don't need autumn or winter this year." It knows that, to survive and thrive, it needs all six seasons and gives each of them the time required.

It's important to focus not only on the quantity, but also on the quality of the time afforded. During one project you may only need a couple of weeks of autumn, but with another you may need to spend six months on your plan in winter, as in writing a book or working on an invention.

Don't take any season for granted. Spend time reviewing with your team whether or not it's fine to move on to the next season. Companies flounder when they try to cut corners. But there's a big difference between efficiency and impatience—and only one of those closes deals.

If not, then go through the cycle again to determine what season or seasons were not executed well.

And there you have the Six-Step Blueprint. This is what nature uses to determine if its produce is up to its standards. Now you can use it with the repeatable success it was intended to do or the repeatable failure if you don't take advantage of every season.

So how can this be used in your business or life? I want to put this in action for you. As I stated in the beginning of this webinar, we are going to go through the steps to determine how to figure out a business's cash flow problems.

As you now know, summer is the external result of all of the seasons working in unison. We've gone through a step-by-step explanation of how nature makes its produce and how it has survived all the years without our intervention.

Summer and winter are opposing seasons and you'll soon learn how they relate to your knowledge and understanding. In summer, you need to know how you're going to use the product or fruit in the next seasonal cycle.

As winter is your inner potential, your fruit is your external potential, waiting to be used. You can see it with your external vision whereas you see winter with your inner eye. It is great to have the fruit but until it is eaten or exchanged for money, it is useless. The same with money. It is useless until it's spent or generating interest.

Your fruit is what you created from your labor; it's the product of your business. Anything that you created falls under this season. You need to have a plan for what you're going to do with it now, how it will help to serve others in the future, and how it can keep fueling you to create more.

This is the maturation season and when you sit down with your client, customer or future boss and show them your product and service and why they should choose you. In summer, decisions are made since it is where knowledge is obtained. Many times deals are held up here because the potential client is deciding to use you or not.

Remember the next season is harvest where you get paid, hired or whatever your goal is to replenish what was lacking or decreased in your business and life. Based on the decision they make in summer, will affect your harvest. Also, here is where you make your decision too, whether to continue the process because it will create a great yield or change your produce

Harvest is needed to create an exchange so you are given the money and the satisfaction you desire. This is the reason why you created your product or service in the first place.

SUMMER EXERCISE (COMPLETION)

Business Questions:

1. Decide if you or others are happy with your product. Notice the feedback you are getting. If all's well, congratulations! You're done with this exercise. If not, move on to question 2.

2. Do you want to change this immediately? Or is it good enough for now? If so, then place the proper sales price on it and start selling. Begin planning on moving into harvest when you can to start replenishing the true reason for creating your product and service in the first place, whether it was for money, to fill a need or a whatever your desire was.

3. If it isn't, why not? How can it be improved? Do you need to bring in outside help or do more market research? Ask questions to your client to see how to help them make the decision to use you.

4. Do you want to end production? Is the product outdated? Is it worth spending any more time on it? Do you no longer want to be in this business?

PERSONAL QUESTIONS:

1. Decide if you are happy with your new personal results. Notice the feedback you are getting from others and is this this the results you wanted? Is it better than expected or not even close?

2. If it is, then what did you do differently so you know how to repeat it in the future?

3. If it isn't, what not? Was it because you did not fully take advantage or work each season to the fullest? Did someone refuse to negotiate with you or disagrees with your new decision or the "new you"?

4. Do you want to end this new result, tweak it so everyone, including you are happy? Are you willing to compromise and are you fully agreeable to this? If not, then re-evaluate.

IMPORTANT NOTE

Be careful when answering these questions. Make sure you're level-headed and not emotionally charged. You don't want to make any decision you'll later regret.

There was a time I almost deleted everything I'd worked on. All of my books, videos, and notes of decades of work. I was frustrated that I couldn't get this off the ground in the way that I wanted. I felt like a failure. But I calmed down. And I am so glad I did.

Make sure to follow each step after analyzing summer's produce so you can continually make the best product and service as possible. This includes you and your personal results you want to achieve.

Stay on course and don't allow other people and things to distract you from reaching your summer's fullest potential.

However, keep in mind — and this is very important — be sure to use the time in summer to enjoy what you've created or helped to create.

CHAPTER FIFTEEN

THE SEASONS DRIVEN BY FEAR

So far, I have discussed how to use the seasons in an inspiring way. I gave you questions to help you view your product through an unbiased lens, inspiring you to continue to improve it or remove it. Of course, you can use these questions regarding any problems or challenges in your life and not only areas pertaining to your business product or service or anything else that pertains to your career.

However, if we really live in a dichotomous world – left/right, up/down, in/out, etc. – then we need to consider how the seasons affect us with an entirely different perspective. This opposing perspective is based on fear.

You may often hear that you need to overcome your fear. You need to beat it so it doesn't beat you. But everyone has a rational fear of something. It's impossible to be entirely fearless and if you have it in your life, you're nothing if not normal.

Before I go into more detail, let's look at the definition of fear. Reviewing definitions from various dictionary references, I've taken the liberty of summarizing the three most important meanings for our purposes:

1. The fear of God, as in reverence and awe
2. Concern
3. Apprehension, fright or distress

The first definition describes a show of respect to a higher power or authority through combination of veneration, wonder, and dread. The second definition is being concerned that you are in danger, which we understand intuitively.

This third definition is pertinent to this chapter. Here, fear means anything from being uncomfortable to being so overwhelmed that you either find it impossible to act or you overly react without thought or feeling. It is the extremes of your actions.

Review the Seasonal Bar Graph below. You'll see it ranges from 1 to 10, with 1 indicating inaction, and 10 an overreaction. The area from 5 to 6, whereby 5.5 is the middle range, is my suggested range for true balanced action.

This is a conceptual graph and I created it for you to better understand this chapter.

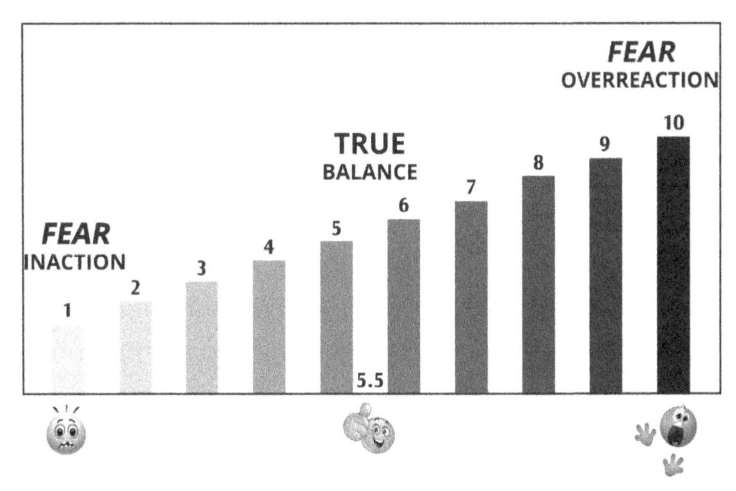

Let's say you know your product or service is not fully ready as you envisioned in the planning stage of winter. The middle range represents your decision to act in truth and not selling it until it can produce the desired results. However, you might choose inaction (fear) and fall to the left of the scale; deciding not to correct this inferiority is a perceived fear of the consequence of modifying it. Maybe you need money immediately and not getting the product out quickly would create a severe decrease in cash flow. Conversely, you might fall to the right of the scale (also fear), perhaps by overstressing about the project. You might be that manager who puts so much pressure on the team to get a project done that everyone ends up being uptight. Both inaction and overreaction are patterns of fear, to the extremes of True Balance.

The side of the range you choose will depend on which side is more comfortable to you in a specific situation. If your boss reacts the same way as your spouse does, you may be stressed about it but may keep quiet and take no action except to say things under your breath. But with your spouse, you overreact and let them have it. Two different reactions, all based on your perception of the consequences to your behavior.

The Seasonal Bar Graph and measuring your reactions relates to being honest with yourself regarding situations at work and in your life that you allow to create stress. By being true to yourself, you don't have to be fearful. Trust yourself to do the right thing for your customers, your business, your family, etc. No matter how your fear manifests, understanding how your perception can mitigate that fear puts you back in the driver's seat. Trust, or being true, is the balance in the middle.

Your perception and/or feelings that trigger your action, inaction, or overreaction indicates how the seasons are motivated, whether through truth or fear.

It's the same for your personal life. What non-truths are you telling yourself and others to avoid the fear of certain consequences?

Let's take a closer look at these opposing terms. I will distinguish each by using the terms, "True" and "Fear" before the name of each season. True is finding the balance while Fear is its opposite.

(1) **True Summer** is the time for you to obtain knowledge by examining your company, product or service. True Summer is using authenticity, accuracy, and certainty to examine your produce with honesty and integrity. It is also the season during which your client gains the knowledge of your product or service in order to decide whether to hire you or not.

Fear Summer is when you are not completely honest with yourself, your boss, or your customers. Is the work that you did for your customer or boss up to par? Did you cut corners? Did you utilize each team member as effectively and efficiently as possible? Did you fully obtain all the knowledge necessary to guide your client or are you winging it? Are you managing out of fear, whether through micromanaging or allowing the inmates to control the asylum?

Fear Summer is illustrated in the earlier example which caused two outcomes -- making a decision too quickly to offer the product or service or not making a decision thus hampering your ability to help someone with it. As the decision maker season, summer can be swayed to either side of the scale.

(2) **True Harvest** is the desire of you and others to take or gather your product for use and to be paid for it. It is the desire to receive something in return for your work. Demanding a fair price for it is a reasonable give-and-take, since both parties are benefiting equally from the product or service. The customer is taking the product and you are receiving payment for it.

This is the same for employees. They are receiving money and other perks to perform and in return you are to get the quality work that was agreed upon.

It is also your acceptance of what you want to change in autumn to bring harmony into your business and your life. True Harvest is valuing yourself enough that you will take or accept what is yours and not undervalue your business or self. This is fully accepting yourself and others without judgement.

True Harvest is for you to replenish what is lacking or decreasing in your business and in your life so that you can give to others in relinquis, and to weather any future pending storms, problems or challenges.

In Fear Harvest, depending on the situation, there is an inequality of exchange based on fear. Your employee may be overworking to meet your demands on the hope you don't hire someone else. You may have someone who is under-performing and you don't let them go due to an underlying fear that doing so will cause more harm to you or your company. This can pertain to your clients as well.

Fear Harvest can cause you to give too much information. Have you ever offered so much information about your service for free in a meeting that the potential client takes what you gave them and never hires you? This season is meant for you to take for you. You devalued your product or service by over-giving without being paid. "This is not that valuable, so here it is for free." The fear results in someone feeling shortchanged.

This fear can cause you to be taken advantage of due to your wanting to please your boss, client, or employee. This is where people become a doormat or get swindled because they are not taking enough for themselves and giving too much.

Fear Harvest is not giving enough to yourself. Often it's connected to someone in your past, especially in your youth, who said taking for yourself was selfish. The same is true for the other side of the spectrum. Overly giving to yourself can manifest in overeating, overworking or in over replenishing your stores in some other way due to a fear of never having enough.

(3) **True Autumn** is where you detach partially or fully from a product or service. You may not fully discard it but will change some of it. You may also dismiss people, things, or events that no longer serve you either in your personal life or your

business. This may be eliminating a marketing director who is not properly marketing the product or decreasing the sale price due to excess inventory. Maybe you realize that a single service within your program is no longer relevant and not serving you or your clients.

Here is another concept for you to think about. Are you accepting anyone as a client or customer or are you qualifying them? And by qualifying them, I mean disqualifying them. By the latter stage of my practice, not everyone became my patient. If they were not fully committed to themselves or the program and did not meet a couple of other criteria, then I would refer them to someone else.

Was it my ego? No! If they were not committed, I saved them money and a lot of stress on both ends. They would not be a good fit for the program. When patients were accepted, the success rates were through the roof. The same applies for my personal and business clientele.

In your personal life, this technique can be used for dating if you are tired of dating the same type of people who annoy you. Just fire them and move on.

When thinking about business, Fear Autumn would be failing to fire an employee who is disrupting your service. This is like the tree keeping and giving life to an infested leaf that is draining its resources and potentially damaging the whole organism. It's your illusory perceptional fear that tells you it is more painful to let this person go than to keep them.

On the other end, you may have received some damaging information about a vendor you have been dealing with for years. Due to fearing that they may do the same to you, you cancel orders and never deal with them again. This decision was based on the assumption the information is true even though you never verified it. Detaching without verifying could cause a loss that could damage you as well.

By detaching from the stress and worry, you can prepare yourself for True Winter.

(4) **True Winter** is the time for you to plan your next move on how to use the information you obtained from summer, your desire to replenish in harvest, and changing in autumn. It is to go within and tap into the following: your knowledge from past experiences; the recommendations of your employees, consultants, accountants, and lawyers; any other professional opinion or expertise. Then, using all that information, you and/or the executive board make decisions and enforce policy.

For those of you who believe in a higher power, this is when you ask for guidance through meditation, prayer, or however you connect, and then trust you will be guided to the right decision. This does not mean that you don't take responsibility. You need to remain aware of any decisions you need to make. It's not saying, "Okay God, I'll check back next Tuesday." As I explained earlier, as in any battle plan, you become aware of the changes that are occurring and allow things to play out and do your best to deter any negative effects.

If you do not believe in a higher power, this is when you must be aware of True Winter and trust in your inner knowledge, your wisdom to stay aware, follow through and make changes when needed.

Fear Winter is you ignoring what you intuitively know will cause harm to your company, your employees or your customers. Maybe it's ignoring your employees who are complaining about that staff member you refuse to fire. Or maybe it's not listening to your consultants or partners about enacting the policies they recommend. Or, conversely, trusting others without doing your due diligence, following what they say without looking at the bigger picture. I can't tell you how many mistakes I made in the early years of my practice because something sounded great and I didn't think about it or research it thoroughly.

This can also happen when you do not trust or have faith in yourself to achieve your desire. This is based on past failures or people in your life that continue to tell you how horrible a person or business owner you are. That includes yourself, too.

This fear can cause you to force things through instead of doing the proper research needed to make a decision instead of just winging it.

(5) **True Relinquis** is the burning desire to open and start your winter plan. This creates the heat to stimulate you to start putting your plan into action, thereby motivating others. This could take the form of encouraging and inspiring your sales force to make sure they have just as burning a desire regarding your service or product.

This is where surrender takes place. Again, if you believe in a higher power, relinquis is allowing forces you cannot see to be attracted into your life. This shows how much trust you have in your higher power by knowing you will be given the patience needed to allow things to occur.

The acorn or the embryo doesn't try to force itself to move it to its goal quicker. It trusts and surrenders to the forces that will open it up, allow it to be fertilized and manifest as a tree or a human.

For those of you who do not believe in a higher power, the blueprint of what is expected in this season gives you knowledge of the expectation. In all examples, your success in this season relies on your patience and tolerance.

Finding the balance between excess patience and tolerance and extreme impatience and intolerance is the key for a successful True Relinquis.

Fear Relinquis is a desire to suppress your giving to others. It's the fear that you would have to open up or be vulnerable to an attack of criticism, rebuke, or defamation. This is where you do not initiate and execute your plan. It's like the flower being scared to open up and show its inner self. It may be your insecurity that you won't do a good job as expected.

Maybe your boss wants you to do a presentation but your fear is so overwhelming you mess it up. Or you could be too patient when expecting a raise, never asking why it hasn't been given to you due to the fear of angering your boss. The fear stifles any sense of urgency, so your boss will wait longer, or possibly never give you the raise.

However, if you have excessively given to others in the past and have been hurt, this fear can cause you to give too much to yourself and become selfish. You are protecting yourself from the outside world because you were taken advantage of too many times. This is when a person who was once very giving becomes a narcissist.

This seasonal fear can cause you to desire to hurt someone's feelings, lashing out and causing many different consequences, for you and for them. Or you may keep your feelings to yourself causing you pain and sorrow. This may later harm your health and moral character. In both examples, an inequality of exchange has occurred due to an excessive or diminished release of thoughts or feelings.

Whether you desire instant gratification or disdain rejection, Fear Relinquis will cause you to feel disharmony in all aspects of your life.

(6) **True Spring** consists of your pollinators: potential clients, financial backers, partners, or others with whom you want to connect in order to create or grow your business. Your desire in True Relinquis to give what was planned in winter results in the motivation to send out signals like flowers do. This means

making phones calls for one-on-one meetings, sending emails to potential or existing clients, and making sure you are expressing your passion while you give your pitch. More deals are closed when your pollinator feels your passion from True Relinquis, your burning desire that has overflowed into your True Spring. This is the building of rapport.

In Fear Spring, you may fail to sufficiently communicate your passion. If you have little passion for what you do or you don't express that passion due to the fear of someone confronting you on its value, and you decrease your chance of building rapport. Your inability to express enough is based on your fear of feeling stupid or embarrassed. This may be the reason why you no longer go to networking meetings because you feel they are not worth your time. That may be true. But could it also be your fear of not rewriting your pitch or communicating differently because those things are much more uncomfortable or not effective any longer?

Conversely, in an attempt not to look stupid or be embarrassed, you may over communicate to your prospects, overwhelming them and causing them to disconnect from you. You may hound them until you get a yes but have you caused just a onetime sale and destroy any chance of a rapport and repeated sales? No rapport will be built because consciously or subconsciously they fear that deciding to hire you would be more painful than doing without your services.

It's a balance of connection. If you tend to over-communicate, try to listen more. If you listen too much, then you need to express yourself more so that your customers aren't forced to try to guess what you are thinking or feeling.

And now you've come full circle. You've returned to summer and are facing the results of how you handled each step with truth or fear. The product of how you handled each season is staring you right in the face. Do you like it or not? Will your client like it? How about your boss?

Here you have a decision to make. Do you use True Summer or Fear Summer? What choice will you make? Will you choose fear and therefore not trust yourself and your team? Regardless, it's all you. You are the one making the decision out of truth or fear.

If you're dissatisfied with your seasonal results, it might be useful to go back to the previous chapters and answer the questions again. Make sure you answer honestly. It's common to cheat the first time around for comfort, so don't beat yourself up about it. But do learn from it. The effectiveness of the seasons depends on your honesty. Do not be afraid to move into the True Seasons. Fear is an illusion that is maintained by power you provide it.

The seasons apply in the same way to your personal life. Are you cheating on your spouse, your taxes, or cheating you or your family out of a fulfilling life? Are you not asking that person on a date out of the fear of being rejected? Are you not taking that vacation out of the fear of losing income or your savings? Whatever the reason, the seasons await you.

Seneca, an ancient philosopher, once said, "The fates lead him who will – him who won't, they drag." I believe the fates are the seasons. They continue to advance whether or not you resist.

The seasons keep moving whether you like it or not. There are times when you have control and others when you do not. Staying in the True Seasons as best as you can will give you the best results.

Remember, the prior season has no meaning to the season you are in right now but was instrumental in getting to the present season. This is why the past, which was your future turned present, is so instrumental in your current state. Don't damn it; embrace it and be grateful for it, for it was a stepping stone to who you are today.

It is just as important not to damn the season you are currently in because of your misperception of what you are expecting out of it. As much as you can see that you are in autumn, the destruction or detachment season, you are also experiencing spring -- its opposite and a growth -- somewhere else. It is your responsibility to perceive the benefit of your current state and not the detriment. It is equally your responsibility to focus on the detriment and not the benefit since all choices are yours.

The trick is to find the balance. One way is to focus on others and give them excellent service and not on what it can do for you. But – and this is important -- feel deserving when things come your way and don't feel uncomfortable receiving them. This way more comes to you when you are unattached to it. Become detached from the outcome you think is best for you and do what is best for all around you. Just as the tree and all nature does.

Have desire for the process and not the outcome. This shifts fear into trust that you are going to be receiving since you are giving. It's a reciprocity. Because you did something good for someone, don't expect them to return the favor, nor should you feel obligated to return the favor if someone is doing something nice for you. You will get a return from someone else. You must because nature is not a one-way street.

When I used to do a lot of community service for the local Chamber of Commerce, I did not get a lot of business from there but it did come from other sources. Once I had stopped the service, I did notice a regression. Once I gave elsewhere, the receiving returned.

When you focus on the goal and not the journey or the process, which is in the moment, what do you do once the goal is achieved? You look for another goal. The goal is the journey; the goal is living in the moment and not for the goal.

Focus only on the goal and you will be disappointed most of your life because there is more to life than achieving the goal. You can be so focused on your goal and not allow shifts to take place because the universe wants to upgrade your goal. Not being aware of it, you could miss out. How many times you said, "Oh man, if I saw that coming, it would have been a whole lot better." Not having awareness and trust in your inner wisdom or your higher power could cause you to miss another upgrade.

This describes the executive, sales professional or employee who is hyper-focused on achieving the bonus or impressing the boss for a new position instead of impressing upon themselves that there is more to life than material things, accolades or tributes.

One of the things I had to learn was to do my best to live in the moment. This moment now, the one as I type these words, are more important right now than finishing this book. Once the book is published, then what? If I did not enjoy this whole process from the first strike of the keyboard to the receiving of my book, my product, my summer, then it would have been treacherous instead of invigorating.

Here's an example a patient of mine who was living in the Fear Seasons in both her business and personal life.

Joanne came to me with an autoimmune disease. During the history intake, she divulged the extraordinary amount of stress she was under. I knew no amount of nutrition, eating right, or exercise would help her until she addressed this.

She attempted to manage her stress, but felt she was trapped in her work. She was a salesperson working for an abusive manager. He would call her and others in the department "stupid," along with other demeaning remarks, and the company was failing to do anything about it. She needed the job so, she reasoned, it felt less painful to be abused than to leave with the possibility of being unemployed for a long time.

Not only was she being devalued by her manager, her home situation was just as demeaning. She didn't have a great relationship with her daughter and her husband reinforced that disrespect. They were devaluing her position as a mother and wife.

When she was able to understand that her Fear Seasons caused her to reinforce her own invalidation, she was able to transfer her energies into the True Seasons. All of the invalidation and pain in her life was a physical manifestation of her own feelings of irrelevance. She attracted people, things, and events to reinforce the very feeling she kept of herself.

Yes, it was true others were devaluing her, knowing they could, on both a subconscious and conscious level. But when she stopped her own self-abuse, and stopped allowing people to take advantage of her kindness with the help of the truthful seasons, she reversed her summer's fruit of invalidation.

Soon after her perception and energy changed, another manager noticed the value of her work for the company. It attracted an opportunity – a pollinator – to make a lateral move within the company. She now enjoys more pay and has more opportunities for others to notice her value and works with a manager who values her opinion and work.

With this change at work, change at home was also happening simultaneously. Her relationship with her daughter improved. Joanne saw how her daughter was devaluing her by not listening and invalidating her authority as a parent. She noticed how she was devaluing her daughter by failing to listen to her opinions when they had reasonable disagreements. What her daughter was doing to her, Joanne was doing as well. Once she stopped the behavior toward her daughter, the arguing stopped and they were able to have a more loving and cooperative relationship.

She noticed her health was also being affected. Taking care of the fear within her in turn changed everything—from diet to exercise, to finding the time for her so that her new validation of herself could be reinforced. With her stress under control, her body could stop causing itself damage. Inflammations from inflammatory thoughts, foods, and drinks she was consuming for comfort were no-win situations. She thought she had no control. But with the simple solution provided by the seasons, she reversed course. She is now enjoying her career, family, and her health—and all of this took place in under a year.

Once she understood of all this, saw the changes taking place, she didn't resist change; she accepted it. This way she no longer regretted the events that took place and looked at them as a gift.

"Life is a series of natural and spontaneous changes. Don't resist them – that only creates sorrow. Let reality be reality. Let things flow naturally forward in whatever way they like," according to Lao-Tse, a Chinese philosopher and writer, and the founder of philosophical Taoism.

You need to understand that nature does not speak your verbal language. It only reacts to your vibration. The vibrations of your thoughts, feelings and actions. I do not care what you tell me what you want. I look at what you have brought into your life that tells me the real story of what you desire. Remember, the outer world is created by your inner world. Sumer is created by winter.

If you do not believe this, then you are telling me in order to change the bitter fruit of the tree, I need to change each apple, not change the inner workings of the tree. It is much easier and truthful to change the tree within then to inject each apple with sugar and pass it along as the real thing.

You are most likely familiar with the words of Jesus, "And I say unto you, ask and it will be given to you, seek and you shall find, knock and it will be opened to you."

This is how you create the fruit you desire. This is what the seasons are all about. Ask, seek, and knock are summer, relinquis and autumn, respectively. Given, opened, and found are harvest, spring and winter.

Ask or invite during relinquis and it will be given to you in harvest. Seek or examine your produce in summer and you shall find the answers within your winter. Knock or penetrate in autumn and it will be opened to you in spring.

Each opposite season is responding to its counterpart. Will you be afraid to use the seasons or trust in the truth of the power that awaits you? It is better to be led with your blessings than to be dragged against your will. Either way, one or the other will occur. You might as well have a say in it.

CHAPTER SIXTEEN

SUMMARY OF THE TRUE AND FEAR SEASONS

The following images will help you gain a better and an even more simpler understanding of each of the seasons and how they create true balance or imbalance through fear.

In the diagram below, **True Seasons Explanation**, I have chosen one word, shown in parenthesis, that explains each season. Summer's decision of what to do with your creation causes you to choose what to do next. Harvest gives you the desire to replenish your stores. Autumn allows you to detach from things that are no longer working for you since you have replenished in harvest. Winter gives you the chance to plan and sequence your steps of your new vision for your future summer.

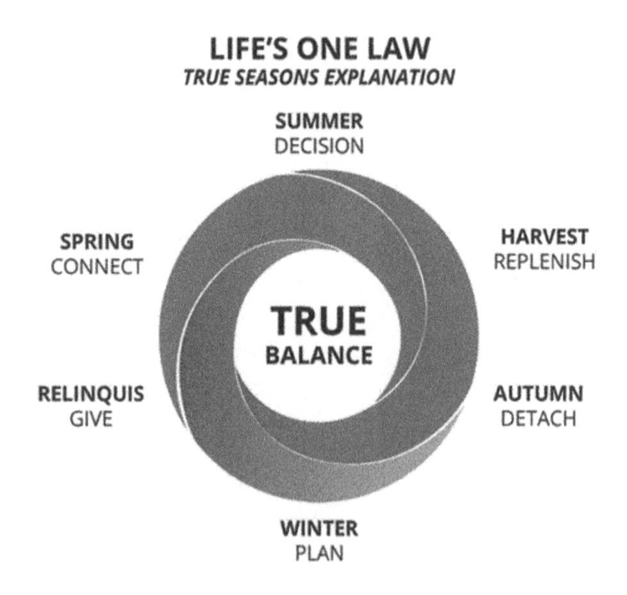

Relinquis allows you the burning desire to open up and give what was created within you to others. Spring brings opportunity to connect with others and create a rapport so they can move in summer and decide to pay you for your creation in harvest, whether it be in money, love or whatever your reasons were to produce. This creates true balance in your business and your life by allowing the seasons to guide you through the process of each step, since each step is just as important as the others.

Conversely, the Fear Seasons explanation show the same words but with opposite arrows on each side. This represents the different degrees as discussed earlier in the Seasonal Bar Graph. The words I will use as examples for the Fear Seasons will be the extremes. It will be up to you to find other synonymous words that describe your particular situation.

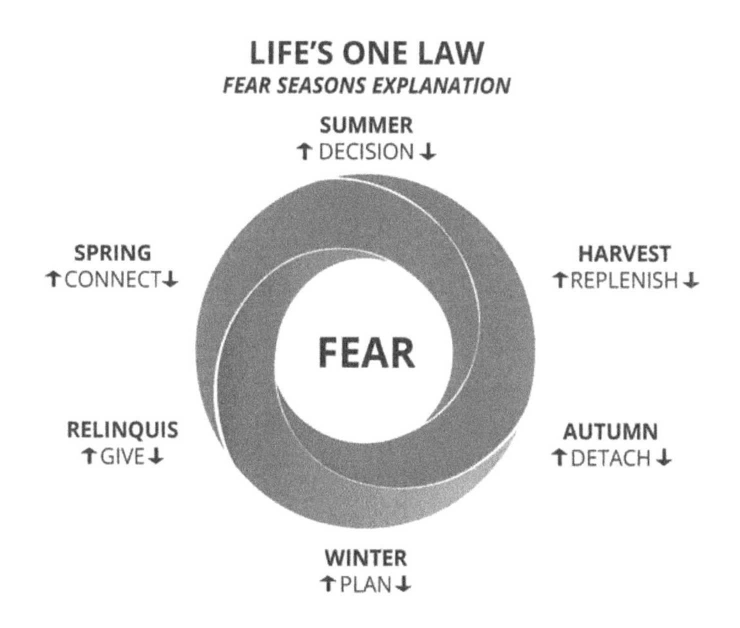

Fear Summer's word "decision" in this case represents your choice of either not making a decision or making quick and rash decisions without thinking them through; this is based on some sort of illusional fear from past decisions. Your Fear Harvest is your desire not to replenish yourself because of your inability to accept from others; this stems from your feeling of not deserving. Conversely, your need in Fear Harvest to over replenish yourself by over eating, over working, using drugs or feeding some other addiction to fill your deleted stores represents what you think is lacking in your life.

When you detach too much in Fear Autumn, it is because you fear certain people, things or events in your life will harm you, so you shun them. Or on the other hand, you may not be able to let go of anything as a hoarder does, in the fear you will not have enough for your winter. In Fear Winter, you do nothing to plan and hibernate from everyone by abandoning any ideas you may have for the future. You may on the other extreme of the scale plan so much that no plan is perfect enough to move into relinquis in order to share with others.

Relinquis' fear may cause you to want instant gratification, giving to yourself too much, causing an imbalance and not feeling the need to share with others. On the other end, overly giving to others can cause them to feel they can leech from you anytime. This can be harmful for both sides as if the ice melts too quickly, it will cause a flood, damaging the crops.

Spring's fear can cause a dependence on others by overly connecting, creating a false feeling of stability and not allowing yourself to do things on your own. Conversely, your inability to connect or confront others because you don't want to feel stupid or embarrassed, causes you to miss out on different experiences and opportunities. These fearful seasons can cause others to judge you and not decide to work with you, or do decide to do so and then take advantage of you.

By remembering each word for each season, you'll have a quick reference of which season you are in and what would be your next move once you decide to stay in fear or move into true balance.

How You and Others Use The Seasons To Interact

You now have a single word to describe each season whether through truth or fear. But how do the seasons affect your interaction with others? Remember, when you are using the seasons, the other person is using them as well. The seasons are interacting with each other. This is true for both personal and business interactions and situations.

While one season is occurring and making more noise to be recognized, its counterpart is there as well. It depends on which one you feel more comfortable focusing. But its counterpart is not only within you, it is being used by the other person as well.

For example, let's say you are a sales person who is talking with a new prospect. You are in the process of qualifying her. What season are you in? Spring, connect, because you are going through the process of creating a rapport with her so she can trust and buy from you.

Your prospect will usually have to answer three questions. Does she need your product? Does her company have the budget to pay for it? Is she the decision maker? If she is the typical new prospect, what season is she in? Autumn. The exact opposite of where you are.

Why autumn? What word in the Fear Seasons Explanation diagram refers to autumn? Detach. Are new prospects eager to buy from you or they do whatever they need to do to breakdown your price, dissect your service, or look for ways to get away from you. These are all autumn characteristics.

If you know that going in, you won't be so surprised that they are not really interested in buying from you or they want to pay you the lowest price (they want a bargain). Don't you do the same thing?

So, what are you to do? Your challenge is to bring them in and show them how their spring is there as much as their autumn. This is why training programs are so important. They teach you how to change the perception of the buyer that you are a flower and they are a bee and there is a win-win for everyone. In the beginning, they are looking at you as an insect eating flower. It's not their job to know the difference. It is yours to show them who you really are.

If you are following the True Seasons, then your prospect will move from autumn into winter (rethink their original plan), be more opened to your expertise (relinquis) and create a rapport (spring) with you. Once this occurs, they will trust (summer) and buy (harvest) from you.

If you are coming at them in any of the Fear Seasons, there's a higher chance they will abandon (winter) the idea to buy from you and release (relinquis) you from their presence since they started in autumn.

I want to make something very clear. Wherever you are on the scale, whether on the opposite end or in the middle, you are where you need to be at that moment in time. Sometimes we need a jolt in our lives to motivate us to start moving in the middle. Sometimes being in the middle is too uncomfortable. Either way, it's not good or bad but just where you are. No judgement, no demeaning yourself. Saying to yourself, "OK. This is where I am, now how do I get to where I want to be?"

This cycle happens with your loved ones, acquaintances and strangers. Everyone and everything is always in a season and the more you are aware of this, the more you can handle any situation.

Being aware of these single words for each season, knowing that both opposite seasons are always present and that you have only control over how YOU think, feel and act with any situation whether through fear or truth, will give you an understanding of what to expect from others.

Can it be this simple? Read on and let's see if it really is.

CHAPTER SEVENTEEN

SELL CONFIDENTLY AND SUCCEED REPEATABLY

This chapter will show you how Nature's Blueprint for Repeatable Success can help you look at selling differently. This is a step-by-step process – changing your perception of sales so you can have more success and less stress while selling.

If there was ever a word that gives business people stress, it's "sell." Unfortunately, the pressure to sell makes sales professionals seem pushy and dishonest.

But the original meanings of words can change or get bastardized. "Sell" is one of them.

The original meaning of sell comes from the Old English, *sellan* and the Old High German, *sellen*, meaning, *to give, furnish, deliver, promise.* It is also related to the Gothic, *saljan*, which means, *to offer a sacrifice.* To sell is to give, not just receive.

The first thing the blueprint recommends is not to focus on the buyer, but on you first. As with previous chapters, we will start with summer.

I will not be going into too much detail here, but I will give you enough to start selling more successfully. Again, the information in this book is only one-third of the blueprint. My trainings and my one-to-one mentoring program go much deeper. For more information, go to my website, **www.dragrios.com**.

STEP 1 - SUMMER

Do you remember what word I used to describe summer? Yes! Decision. When contemplating selling, you need to make a decision. What is your intent in selling to this person? This is a great starting question because it clears up your purpose for calling on this person. Do you need this sale because you need to pay your bills or is your perception of your intent to give or offer them a service? This sets your intent or the real meaning of your call.

After focusing your intent, here are some other summer questions to start asking yourself:

1. Is my product or service a good fit for this buyer?

2. If not, how can I specialize it for them? What different offers do I have to present? (You will determine their specific needs in another season. For now, you should do your homework on this buyer, i.e. website, internet, other buyers they use or have used in the past, etc.)

3. Write down three potential problems the buyer may be experiencing.

Summer starts your strategy, the objective for meeting the client. It takes into account your true reason for selling--clearly and concisely, not just winging it.

As long as you are clear on your intentions and your attention is on truth and not fear, then you can go into the next season to see how you feel about your motive. I write more about service in Chapter 23.

STEP 2 - HARVEST

Harvest is the season of replenishment in which the tree takes for itself. Harvest reveals how you feel about your product, service, or offer to the buyer.

How you feel about something is the duty of harvest. It is where value is generated. How valuable do you feel your product or service is to this buyer? We already know how valuable it is to you if you sell it, but taking notice of how you feel about your product in the moment of selling can easily be overlooked. If you sit in quiet before you start selling, you set the mood of the sale — positive or negative.

Harvest is the taker. Are you willing to take or accept the responsibility to sell with the utmost of integrity so you will feel good about the relationship you have with your future buyer?

How valuable do you feel? Giving value to yourself first and building up your self-worth, will be felt by the buyer. This can be subconscious or conscious.

This build up is not being selfish, but self-nourishing (Chapter 6). Only you can rely on you to nourish yourself. This keeps you in control instead of waiting for others to value you.

An exercise you can do is put yourself in their position and feel what the buyer must be going through. Ask yourself, "I wonder how they may be feeling about their problem?" Maybe their job is on the line and they can't make a buying mistake, so they are already in a defensive mode. There are thousands of scenarios they could be going through. Taking a moment to empathize can make you more approachable during the meeting. Tap into your past experiences to remind you of what they may be feeling.

Harvest questions to ask are:

1. Do I really feel my product or service is right for this buyer?

2. Do I emanate confidence and success or desperation and worry?

3. If I feel anything other than valuable, to myself and my potential buyers today, what happened earlier today or in the past that made me feel this way? (By taking notice of your mood and the triggers that caused you to feel anything other than confidence, happiness and a willingness to serve, you can shift your success.)

A very important question you should ask yourself from time to time is, "Do I value what I am selling?" Not valuing your product or service is a good sign you don't value yourself. If you did, you would not be selling something you don't believe in. You may not be able to quit your job at this time or sell something else. What you can do meanwhile is find something valuable within your current product or service and sell that until you can find something you feel good about.

The product or service may be valuable but it could be that you are not successful in selling it. You may also be projecting unsuccess onto the product instead of upon how you think and feel about it. If you are, then go back to the questions in Chapter 8 and start finding the truth of your feelings about yourself, your business and your life.

Once you become aware of why you are selling your product or service (summer) and how you feel about it (harvest), autumn is there for you to detach from anything or anyone that is no longer serving you, including your behaviors that lead to unfavorable consequences.

STEP 3 - AUTUMN

Autumn is detachment. When the tree prepares for winter, it does not need to be giving precious energy to leaves or fruit. Would a meeting with a potential buyer be more effective with low confidence or with a valuable reason to sell, fulfilling your needs as well as the needs of the buyer?

In this season you use different action steps to change your thoughts and attitude, to improve your rapport with the buyer. This is a good time to release any false beliefs, negative thoughts toward someone who might have made you upset earlier or any thoughts on how the meeting will go due to the rank of the buyer (e.g., CEO, etc.).

Do not concern yourself with outcomes just yet. Just be focused, have a true smile on, and let things unfold as if you did not need this sale. This allows any resistance or negative feelings that might be present to dissipate. It creates a natural, less stressed, and non-intrusive environment that you and the buyer can enjoy. Even if the buyer is stressed out, I have seen many times when the seller is in a relaxed and confident state, the buyer's state changes and the deal happens.

Here are some autumn questions you can ask yourself before your meeting:

1. Do I feel any resistance within me? Do I have any doubts or ill feelings clouding my true reason to sell?

2. Have I analyzed and recently reviewed the information I obtained regarding the buyer (summer) and any other information that will help me guide the buyer to making the best choice for them?

3. During the meeting, continually review and detach from any old or new thoughts and feelings that will derail you from your main purpose -- to sell by giving your best to the buyer and fulfilling their needs.

Autumn continuously analyzes your situation for any change while encouraging you to respect yourself and the buyer.

STEP 4 - WINTER

The knowledge that you obtain in winter gives you valuable information in order to supply your buyer what he or she needs.

Within winter selling, there are three sub-steps. There are also three sub-parts to the other seasons as well, but I will not review them here.

Remember from Chapter Eleven that winter questions are seeking knowledge within or the knowledge that is hidden from you. Your buyer has the information of what they need and how to influence them. They will gladly give it to you if you ask the right questions. By following this sequence of questioning, you will have a better chance of obtaining it.

The Three Types of Questioning for Winter

The P.I.C. Method

Positioning Questions

Positioning questions give you the ability to understand the position or predicament of the buyer or company. Their past decisions, usually a sequence of decisions over days, months, years or decades, have placed them in such a position that they need your help to move forward.

Position questions are usually the ones buyers don't like to answer. These are usually questions about how their business is being run, how old their equipment is, how many employees do they have. Questions that give you the understanding of the buyer's business.

This is the same as when you go to your doctor's office. This is your intake form. The questions you hate to fill out. Well, this is the buyer's hatred. Doing your homework in summer would get you a lot of this information elsewhere. It would also impress the buyer that you took the time and an interest in their company.

If you are chronically ill and you go from specialist to specialist, think about how many intake forms you would have to fill out by answering the same questions. This is what the buyer has to do when they're dealing with a chronically ill business or machine, and has many different sales professionals call upon her in a day or month. So, keep it brief, because, even though important, these questions are not the most effective ones to get the sale.

Interruption Questions

These questions allow you to discover what obstacles, problems and challenges the buyer has that caused their business to be interrupted. Depending on what you are selling, by understanding what decisions caused the interruption in their workflow and what decisions they used to try to correct it that didn't work, shows you just how you can help them.

Interruption questions can start off as:

1. What difficulties are you having with ___?
2. What stops you from having success with ___?
3. Who or what is causing your ___?
4. What concerns do you have with ___?
5. Who or what is holding you back from ___?
6. What does your staff say about the effectiveness of ___?

Interruption questions allow you to start gathering the materials that have created their obstacles.

Connection Questions

These questions allow you and the buyer to figure out together what caused these painful consequences and how your product or service is the connection they need to bail them out. If you can get them to figure this out without you telling them, that is even more powerful because then it was their idea and not yours.

These questions start creating a picture for them to see that their pain will worsen if they do nothing or not buy from you.

This is why I named it P.I.C. – like the shorthand for "picture." This is what you are doing in winter. Remember, winter is your vision or picture of your future summer, the commitment of the sale or the close. You are sequentially creating a picture to bring to mind their problem so when you offer the solution, they will be much more receptive.

Connection questions are:

1. How does this affect your effectiveness with or in ___?
2. How much money has it cost your business by not ___?
3. If you have this (their answer from Interruption Question), doesn't that create ___?
4. If you were to eliminate this (problem), what would that mean to you?
5. What you are telling me is, you have (problem) and it has been happening over a long period of time. If you do nothing about it, it would cause...?
6. So, if I am understanding this correctly, what you are saying is (summarize and reveal the picture your questioning has revealed.) Is this correct?

The last question is your summary of their previous summer, the dilemma you want to solve for them. It takes something that was abstract and applies meaning. Meaning creates a boundary around problems and solutions. It makes it even more real for them.

Winter is the fact-finding. You don't start gardening when it's 10 below. Instead, you contemplate what you will do in summer. Hold off your solutions or telling them the benefits of your product or service until you know you have created a picture that the buyer now understands and has confirmed.

If you did your job in winter, they can't dispute it. But there will be buyers who may still dispute it because they don't want to see how bad it is. They allowed it to get so bad, they may think the solution will be more painful.

I saw this behavior when I treated chronically ill patients. I would come across patients who would get upset because I painted a picture of their life. Other doctors, usually specialists would only focus on the area they specialized in. But with me, I showed how all of their systems in the body were affected, the damage it caused them and what it would look like if they did nothing.

I did this so they would be able to change their outcome. No one can change anything until they take responsibility for it.

STEP 5 - RELINQUIS

Relinquis is the giving season. It is here the flower opens up and shows its potential pollinators what it has to offer. Now is the time for you to show the buyer what you have to offer and not any sooner.

Do you remember what the original definition of selling is? To give! When you actually sell, this is the season you do it in. Winter is usually cold and icy. Nature uses relinquis to start melting the ice, the barrier it put around the life-giving water that is trapped inside.

If you were successful and fully completed winter in the way I described, then you would have shown the buyer the barrier they placed around their problem. Just like nature, you use relinquis to start melting that barrier with the description of your product or service, so the problem can be freed.

Relinquis puts value on your product and service. This is a value driven season, just like harvest. Asking questions that are solution-oriented solidifies to the buyer that you have the answer he or she has been looking for all this time. Some may not even know they were looking for an answer. These questions make them feel the pain and want to do something about it.

In winter, you are not the only one opening up. They are too. You exposed their wants and needs and their desire to fix it.

Don't hesitate to offer a solution they did not express to you. If they are truly opened, they will welcome the suggestion. But be careful – it could be perceived as an oversell and then they will close up like a clam. This is where experience selling plays a role.

Relinquis questions can be:

1. If I understand this correctly, you need for ________ to happen and if you had ________, that would solve your problem, correct?

2. Why do you feel having this (seller's solution) would make (problem) more efficient and less costly?

3. By replacing this (machine or procedure), how much money would you save monthly? Yearly?

4. If this is as important as you are expressing to me, wouldn't having (your product/service) make this all worthwhile and a big relief to you and your company?

5. Wouldn't (seller's product/service) make you work differently, getting you out of the office on time and enjoying the things you love to do?

6. How useful would it be to you if you were able to no longer have the stress of this (problem)?

These questions build value which in turn makes them feel better. Feelings are not defined. They are a vibration that emanates from you, so you are trying to bring a positive feeling to them. Relinquis is about making them and you feel good about the deal that is being presented.

STEP 6 - SPRING

Spring is when potential pollinators come and fertilize the flower. It's where things happen between two parties to join for a common cause. This is where relationships are formed and solidified, depending on each party's needs.

Spring is where you demonstrate what you, your product or service can do. This is mating season in full swing. This is where you show how your solution connects the dots for them.

If the buyer says yes during the demonstration and you have not finished, STOP! Don't show any more. This is where sales can be lost.

Spring is expression through some sort of communication. They may express that they want to buy. Some sales take more than one meeting. You may have to meet their boss who makes the final decision. This season is also where they can disconnect and end your relationship by not buying from you.

There are no specific questions to ask in this season except to make sure that your demonstration is making sense to them, that you are not over or under doing it, and that they have seen enough.

STEP 7 – SECOND SUMMER

Second summer is the commitment step – the decision by the buyer to buy or not. Commitment is a promise or an obligation to do business. Obligation in the way that they are taking responsibility for the transaction and decided to trust your product and service (and you) to do what you said it and you could do.

Remember summer and winter are perception seasons. In winter, they perceive their problem to be real and in summer, they perceive that your solution is their answer. When you change their perception, you can actually have them commit and complete the deal before you even ask them for the sale.

If you did not change their perception, then one or more of the steps just explained were not fully completed or the buyer was not serious, had no money and was shopping around. But this is never a waste of time. This is where you go back to your first summer and think of the kind of prospect this buyer was. Did you perceive them differently than they actually were? Maybe you are calling on anybody instead of doing your homework and picking the buyers that are right for you. This process makes you a more experienced sales professional. This is how you evolve.

There will be many reasons why a buyer will or will not commit to the sale. For example, it could be related to how to handle the size of the sale.

When I was treating patients who had insurance and a small co-pay, there was not too much to talk about. People would start treatment because the money risk was low. If they started treatment and it didn't work for them, then the loss was manageable.

But when managed care came along and people had larger deductibles and co-insurance because I did not participate in-network, I had to express the value of what I was doing compared to someone else. How they would save money.

Then when I moved into functional medicine, where insurance did not pay for any of my services and the price for my program was much more substantial, I had to really focus on their needs. I had to get specific and explain how my unique treatment was the solution for them, to be clearer and demonstrate the benefits so I had a better chance of helping that particular patient.

But my policy was also that I did not accept everyone as a patient. If I felt that they would not be committed to the program, then why should they start? It would only end poorly. It's the same for my clients now.

So, with higher priced sales, you will need to spend more time in winter and relinquis and make sure you paint that picture very clear in winter (P.I.C.). Ask more questions in relinquis so they feel you can help them. Then it will be easier to demonstrate your solution and for them to commit to you.

This way you both move from second summer into harvest where an exchange takes place. You are replenished with money and they will take your product and service.

CONCLUSION

Now you have a blueprint to follow to sell and give to those existing and potential buyers your product or service to make their lives easier and better. Isn't this the true reason you sell? It is to give so you can receive not only monetarily, but also the knowledge of making a difference in people's lives.

Here's one simple rule to keep in mind while applying the blueprint to selling. Many people don't want to see how their decisions created the mess they are in. They may not want to know how much money they lost because of it or may feel embarrassed for allowing it to occur. Some may not think it's serious.

In some cases, no matter how you sell or how you use the blueprint, you may never get the sale. You are only responsible to the buyer, not for them. It is their ultimate decision to decrease or eliminate their pain.

But just because the buyer said no, does not mean they rejected the whole you. They just rejected your product or service at that moment in time. Keep a good relationship with them because in six months, their perception may change. I saw this with many patients who originally said no and then called me later after they tried the route they thought was best for them. Never judge anyone. In the end, if you were meant to help them, they will show up again.

Remember, how you choose to use a season, whether in fear mode or in truth, will create a drastically altered outcome.

The previous chapters provided the insight into life's essential fairness. Nature loves balance, and imbalance is just an opportunity to make a correction or create a different experience for you to evolve. The reason you might feel this isn't the case is because no one had yet given you the rules of the game.

The frustrating part is not that we face challenges. I believe we want "simple," but we don't want "easy." We all strive after meaningful and rewarding pursuits. If life was going well no matter what you did, and you never had a challenge, it wouldn't be long before you were in my office complaining that life is so boring.

What is more invigorating? An easy sale or a sale that over time prevailed?

Remove the villain from the movie and how long will you watch it? Do the same for the defensive line and see how exciting the game is when the running back is sprinting down the field with no one chasing him.

The true frustration is not challenges or conflicts, but not knowing the simple rules of the game we call life. It's hard to know when to turn right or left, to navigate in the direction of the people and things that will help us create a better life, when no one gives you the information.

I just gave you a glimpse into the rules of the game of life – the six seasons. Knowing how to use them makes the pursuit of your goals simpler, more quickly rewarding, more focused, and more fun. The more you study, understand, and use the six seasons, the faster you will succeed.

But what if I told you that there was even a faster way than the six seasons? A shortcut within them that can make some things manifest faster and simpler? I want to share that shortcut with you. The rule of rules that I call *Life's One Law*.

SECTION SUMMARY

1. The six seasons when used as outlined in this section, will help you solve any problem, whether personal or business. Take a problem you are having, start with summer and answer the questions pertinent to your problem. Make sure each step is fully implemented and then go to the next step.

2. If you feel uncomfortable or stressed performing a step, then review the fear associated with that season under the Fear Seasons to understand why.

3. Then use the True Season of that step to neutralize it.

SECTION 4:
LIFE'S ONE LAW

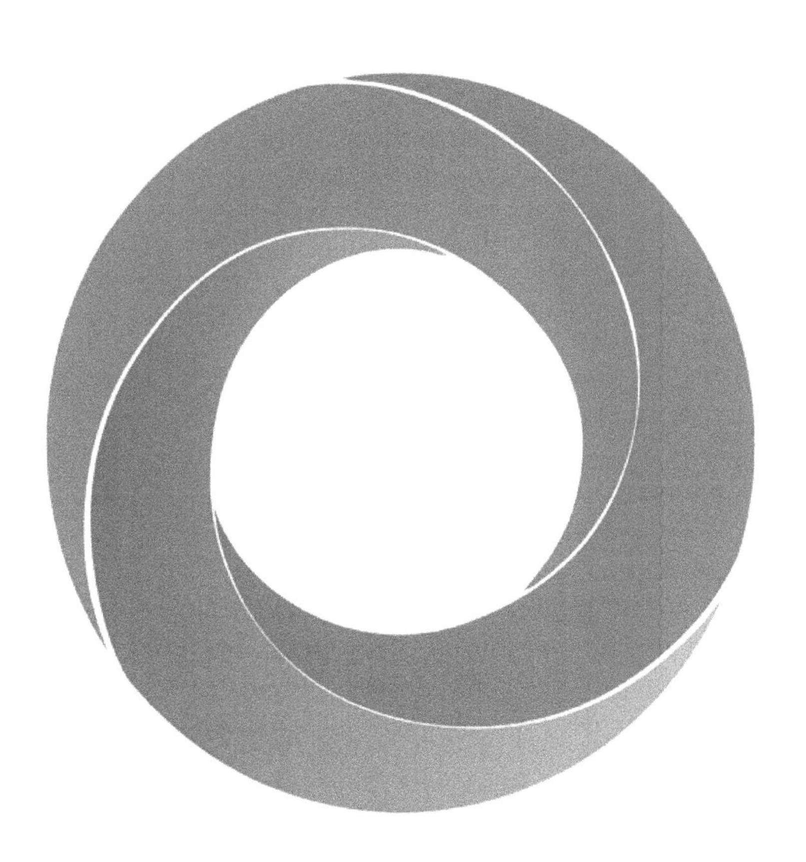

CHAPTER EIGHTEEN

CAN LIFE BE THIS SIMPLE?

It has been shown that the changing of the seasons is driven, in part, by the revolution of the Earth around the Sun.

Here's the question important for us to consider: What changes the seasons within us? How can we be going through winter in one part of our lives and harvest in another? Is it the revolutions of the Earth or something else that affects everything that exists?

Why would knowing this affect the bottom line of your business, attract high performing employees and allowing everyone involved to be as happy as they can be while serving your customers?

In these next few chapters, I will give you a method to improve your business that is even *simpler* than the seasons.

When I first discovered the six seasons, I thought this was the way nature worked and there was nothing else.

I was wrong.

When I was starting the seasons diagram, spring and autumn had opposite functions. One built while the other destroyed. It occurred to me that enzymes – those proteins in our body – were the perfect example for explaining the function of these seasons. Enzymes build and destroy. They link and unlink.

I found something in nature which is one structure with two seemingly opposing functions that matched the functions of spring and autumn perfectly. I found other structures that followed the course of the seasons as well. Then, it hit me: *we* do the same things, depending on the situation.

I noticed that each season and its complement were two halves of a larger whole—summer/winter (S/W), harvest/relinquis (H/R), and spring/autumn (S/A). While testing and retesting my discovery in treatment with thousands of patients, I saw I could explain the basic function of the combined seasons with one word. I was able to supplement with one functional word that could explain each of the seasonal combinations: Director (S/W), Supplier (H/R), and Communicator (S/A).

The opposite seasons when combined were governed by three basic words, or principles. Each principle explained beautifully every action the opposite seasons portrayed. I looked at the fundamental makeup and behaviors of planets, atoms, animals, insects, and many other things that exist in the universe. All followed these embodying principles.

I was even more convinced when I looked at what makes up the human body. Briefly, we are made up of three germ layers called the ectoderm, the mesoderm, and the endoderm. To my amazement, each germ layer's functions could be explained with one of these three words. No matter where I looked, I started to see that everything and everyone followed these three simple principles.

I sat back. *Can it be that simple?*

But the longer I explored the idea and tested my hypothesis, the more I saw that these three principles were at the core. Moreover, I found that the principles could not be separated. They were interdependent upon each other, just as the ectoderm, which makes the nervous system, sensory organs and other structures cannot properly function or even *exist* without the other germ layers.

This meant the three principles were truly three parts of *one*.

And the only thing that could adequately explain the *three-in-one* principles which I saw emerging in all things was the following: "A statement of fact, deduced from observation, to the effect that a particular natural or scientific phenomenon always occurs if certain conditions are present."

That definition is of the word *LAW*.

The three principles created just one law!

It seems to make sense that if we're made up of the same particles as the stars and the planets, we should follow the same principles or rules as them. After all, why would there be a separate set of principles for us? And there aren't.

But one law can't exist by itself. Like the cells in our body, it's fair to say they make up who we are—but only as they work together, not as individuals. We can look at each cell individually, but when we step back and look at the cell as part of an organ we have a different perspective. Its individuality no longer exists. Similarly, there are multiple parts to the one law, just like there are multiple parts to us.

I have called my law ***Life's One Law***. It's comprised of the *three principles*:

- The Director Principle
- The Supplier Principle
- The Communicator Principle

Therefore, *Life's One Law*, comprised of three basic principles, governs everything in the universe including all human behavior. As you may know, our behavior is made up of characteristics or traits. It is here I would like to explain to you how each of our traits are governed by these three principles.

Let me give you a clearer picture of this.

The three traits are broken down in this way:

- The Dominant Trait or the 'Go-To' Trait
- The Less Dominant Trait or Mediator Trait
- The Non-Dominant Trait or The Sabotaging Trait

The Dominant Trait is the one you most often use. It's your *go-to* trait in times of stress, no matter the stress' magnitude. That is why during similar circumstances your reaction will also be similar.

The next trait is called the Less-Dominant Trait, or the Mediator Trait. This is the bridge between your Dominant Trait and your Non-Dominant Trait, or the Sabotaging Trait .

The Sabotaging Trait is *non-dominant* because it represents the part of us we don't pay attention to—we aren't aware it's there and we definitely don't know how it is affecting us on a daily basis. We are internally programmed to rely on the other two traits, mainly the Dominant Trait, and as a result we don't realize the Sabotaging Trait is trying to get our attention by attracting inefficiencies (stress) in our lives to wake us up to the imbalances we have created or have allowed to be created.

It's like the old adage, "The squeaky wheel gets the oil." You will pay more attention to your Dominant Trait because it is more prominent in your life. The discovery of your Sabotaging Trait allows you to become aware of the other wheel. Even though it may not be squeaking, doesn't mean it doesn't need attention.

It's the same regarding your dominant and non-dominant hands. Let's say you are right handed. You use that hand for almost everything. You are comfortable with it. Now, let's say you injure your right hand. How awkward will it be to be forced to use your left hand? Perhaps so frustratingly awkward that you would still try to use your right hand, no matter how painful. Using both hands equally reduces the chance of overworking your dominant hand.

The same applies to your traits. Using your comfortable trait (the Dominant Trait) especially in situations of stress, is more comfortable than acting differently (the Sabotaging Trait). Learning to act, instead of react, to stress causes you to be more balanced in handling different types of situations.

When you hear the word *sabotage*, you think of underhanded interference in more of a negative connotation. However, there is a positive attribute of this word. To fully understand this, we need to investigate the origin of this word.

The French word *sabotage* was coined in the 1890s by the anarchist Émile Pouget. This can be found in the book *Syndicalism, Industrial Unionism and Socialism* (1913) by the socialist and labor reformer John Spargo.

Pouget recommended to labor unions that workers slowdown and create inefficiencies. He came up with the noun *sabotage*. It was based on the French verb *saboter*, which originally meant, *to make loud clattering noises with wooden shoes*. Peasants who wore heavy wooden shoes would walk around more slowly and carefully.

I am using this term in its original meaning. The Sabotaging Trait creates conflicts, challenges and problems or inefficiencies in your life to make you slow down. Other synonymous terms would be, *to tinker* or *shake up*.

This trait creates resistance not to punish you but to shake things up in your life and business so you can evolve and grow, or dissolve through fear. It's your choice again. It tries to get your attention in this way to show the imbalance.

Think about this. If you had no inefficiencies in your life, whether big or small, and everything came easy to you, you would be bored because there would be no challenges.

I think the biggest misunderstanding with many people is that they think that life should have no problems. It is in my opinion, we are here not to learn but to experience fully what this life has to offer. It is through the Sabotaging Trait we get to experience this.

But because you do not know too much about it, you rely on your Dominant Trait and Mediator Trait to get through the madness, increasing stress until you finally slow down and maybe, just maybe, figure out why this keeps repeating in your life and your business.

In failing to recognize and use the Sabotaging Trait, we cause ourselves to continually react instead of act—the true cause of our life challenges. But before we can use it, we must know what it is.

For example, here are the thoughts of one of my patients, Joe, who wanted to control his anxiety:

> "I have anxiety and it can get so debilitating that it causes me to be paralyzed where I don't want to do anything. I get disorganized and don't get things done because my main fear is making a mistake. I don't want to look like an idiot. So, I avoid doing many things. This has caused so many problems not only in my personal life but at work.
>
> "As I learned how these traits affected my behavior, I realized I was using my Dominant Trait mainly to react to my stress. It would work occasionally but most times using my Dominant Trait would cause me more anxiety. When I discovered my Sabotaging Trait was the main cause of my unfavorable outcomes, I felt more

in control. It just made so much sense to me that I only had to focus on this."

Everything starts with one step. As humans, we either act or react, suggesting we handle our problems in a favorable or unfavorable way. This can lead to growth or reduction, success or failure.

I have found that our course of action is driven by these three traits and whatever action you personally choose always causes a reaction in kind.

This is like two sets of dominoes—each set creating a favorable or unfavorable result. One by one, consequences of that first choice begin to mount, creating a path of repeating or similar results. Depending on which domino you push, you get different results, either of desperation or inspiration. The decision to push can trigger an emotional reaction of anger and despair, or joy and happiness. I call it the *Behavior Domino Effect*.

Plato said, "Human behavior flows from three main sources: desire, emotion, and knowledge." He had it right. The three principles – supplying our desire, communicating through our emotions, and choosing which direction we want to move based on our knowledge – create our behavior and flow effortlessly from this domino effect.

Unfortunately, we often aren't aware which domino will cause which chain reaction when we're presented with the decision.

However, I discovered the first domino that leads to actions of desperation and failure. This is your *Sabotaging Trait.* This trait is how you typically protect yourself from whatever you think is harmful to your existence, success, or growth. The trait puts you onto a safer course, consciously or subconsciously.

Once you understand your Sabotaging Trait, you will be aware of how to push the domino that leads to inspiration. It starts with a one sentence solution called your *Antidote*. This is how you can find a new path to turn your life around. It leads you to a clearer understanding of how to consistently act differently—how to recognize your Sabotaging Trait is warning you there is an imbalance.

What you will find is that your Sabotaging Trait and its Antidote are the opposite of each other. Just like the seasons and their individual complements. By discovering and understanding both, you will be able to make a conscious choice and be absolutely certain of the outcome of each action.

Once Joe was given his Antidote, and performed his one simple favorable action step, his anxiety decreased dramatically. He has learned how to live *better*.

Discovering your Sabotaging Trait will make you aware of how the imbalances in your life are created so you can balance them out.

Adversity is always the best teacher. Your Sabotaging Trait is trying to get your attention so you can focus on the imbalances in your life and turn your protection into growth and evolve.

In the next chapter, I am going to explain to you how the three principles work together with the three traits so you can clearly understand how we develop success or failure.

CHAPTER NINETEEN

THE SABOTAGING TRAIT AND ITS ANTIDOTE

The Sabotaging Trait is uncovered by realizing the order in which you use all three traits. I call this your *Personality Stress Sequence,* and it will enlighten you on exactly how you respond to your stresses.

Your Dominant Trait, Mediator Trait, and Sabotaging Trait give you insight into how you run your business, make sales, or hire staff. They will also show how you make decisions in your personal life, how to interact with people and how you handle your challenges.

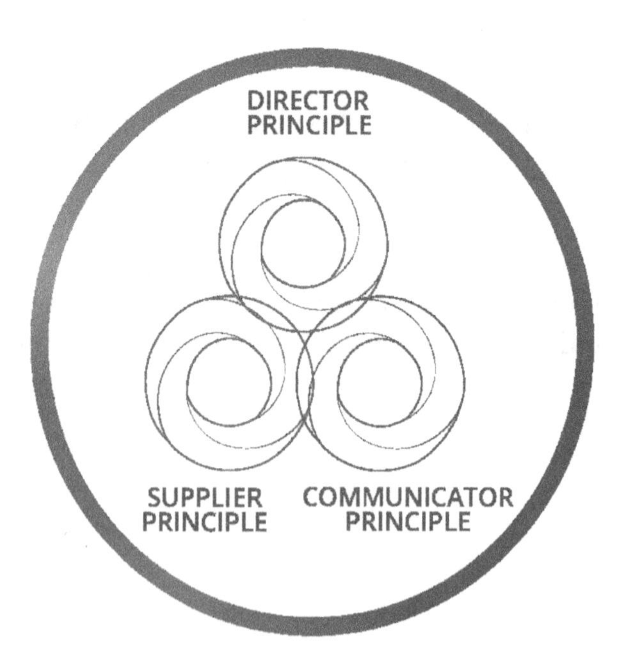

The three principles govern each of your traits depending on your Personality Stress Sequence. Your thoughts, feelings, and emotions all depend on which principle represents each trait. This then drives your actions and reactions in different situations.

Let's look at the structure of *Life's One Law*. The diagram here shows three small circles or mobius strips within a larger circle. This mobius strip is the same one I used as a central part of the illustration in the six seasons cycle images, as well as for my logo. I chose to use a mobius strip because it purely represents *Life's One Law*. It's a continuous one-sided surface formed from a rectangular strip by rotating one end 180° and attaching it to the other end. While it may appear that you are looking at different sides, it is the same side. An insect can walk on the strip indefinitely and end up at the same place it started. Although it may look like it's made up of three sections, it is really the same strip and you are looking at the same side.

It illustrates that you may be seeing one season, but if you look at it from another perspective, its opposite is right there as well. The three sides represent the three principles which together represent *Life's One Law*. They are all one. (To see this in color, please go to www.dragrios.com/images)

Getting back to the diagram, these three mobius images are within a larger circle. The outer circle represents *Life's One Law*. Again, the smaller equally-sized mobius images represent each part – the three principles – that make up *Life's One Law*.

The top mobius image corresponds to The Director Principle, the bottom left image to The Supplier Principle, and the bottom right image to The Communicator Principle.

The three mobius images are the same size because one principle is no more important or powerful than the other. They are *equivalent*. You can start with any principle and move in any direction. All three rely on one another.

We use these principles in a particular sequence so we can exist, especially when we are under stress. They make up who we are and govern our every thought, feeling and emotion.

Working together, they act as one law – *Life's One Law.*

THE PRINCIPLES AND YOUR TRAITS

Life's One Law and its parts rule every aspect of who you are—they are your *traits*. Traits are the principles applied *personally*, since they govern or rule your behavior. Therefore, the Director Principle is equivalent to your Director Trait, the Supplier Principle to your Supplier Trait, and the Communicator Principle to your Communicator Trait. The sequence of these traits makes up your specific Personality Stress Sequence which affect your *thoughts*, *feelings,* and *emotions,* respectively.

What's fascinating is that each principle is interchangeable with each of your traits. Therefore, your thoughts follow the Director Principle, your feelings follow the Supplier Principle and your emotions follow the Communicator Principle. A summary of each relation looks like this:

Director Principle = Director Trait = Thoughts

Supplier Principle = Supplier Trait = Feelings

Communicator Principle = Communicator Trait = Emotions

Thoughts correspond to your Director Trait, which follows the Director Principle. What do thoughts, the Director Trait, and this principle have in common? A direction needs a director. What is the main function of our thoughts? They're there to direct. Our mind directs and commands our body and everything within it.

Your Director is your decision maker. It takes control and chooses your path in life. No matter what situation arises, the director part of you takes control and decides what to do.

The two components of the Director are *awareness* and *follow through.*

You choose things based on your perception and your perception is determined by your knowledge and understanding of similar past experiences. By using the first component of the Director – by *becoming aware* of your perception of people, things, and events – you gain control.

Here's an example: If you meet someone who reminds you of your ex, you become aware of that similarity and it influences your interpretation of that person's character. If you had a bad experience in that relationship, you can, with knowledge and awareness, decide to disengage from interacting with the person who reminds you of your ex. But without actively putting that awareness to use, you will likely fall into the same sort of damaging relationship as you had with your ex. The director in you has been persuaded to make certain decisions based on whether or not you are aware that someone is influencing you.

That's why the second component is *follow through* -- because it controls whether or not you stay on course when using your awareness.

If you need to finish a project for work but your friends want you to go out, you have two choices. You can either follow through on your plan to finish or decide to go with your friends. In being aware of your commitment and following through on your plan to finish the project, your perception changes. You can take control of your life and decisions. You can actively change your reality from a bad consequence (getting reprimanded at work) to a good one (praise for finishing the project).

Through awareness and follow through, you *control your reality*. Your reality is your inspired or desperate *thought* process. You chose it. No one else.

Therefore, the Director Trait is made up of your thoughts. But they need something to direct, a supply of some sort. This supply is your feelings. They fuel your thoughts regarding the people, things, and events which come into and out of your life. Since the Supplier Principle and your Supplier Trait are the same, this trait governs your feelings.

When you have a thought, if there is no real feeling or desire fueling it, then the thought will usually go away. However, if there's feeling behind a thought – a feeling of hunger, for instance – you will be energized to put it into action. This desire is for an exchange of some sort, a give and take. In our example, you give your hunger and take in nourishment.

The two components of the Supplier are to *give* and *receive*. The Supplier Principle is balanced when there is an even flow of these two actions.

The basic element that makes up your supply of people, things, and events is *energy*. When you have a *feeling* of hunger, you are *supplied* with the *energy* to find food.

As humans, we are made up of energy. From the people and things around us and the events that we create – everything is energy.

Life's One Law determines what happens to that energy—where it goes, how it's used, and what it affects. The three principles explain individually how energy is directed, supplied, and communicated. Since we are energy, it in fact explains our behavior.

As per the laws of physics, energy is neither created nor destroyed. We transform or exchange it.

When you work, you use energy which is exchanged for money. With that money, you buy things. The energy of work indirectly gets transformed into or exchanged for other things. This is why the basic characteristic of our Supplier Trait is to give and receive.

Whenever you give, you receive at the exact same time. As explained in Chapter 7, when I give you a gift and you give nothing in return, in reality you have given me the opportunity to feel happy. Rejecting your gift gives me the opportunity to be sad. This action happens simultaneously.

Therefore, the basic thing that we supply each other is our feelings. They're energy like anything else. Every person, thing, or event that comes into your life has a particular feeling attached to it. We might feel good about it, bad, or even indifferent. The point is that we're always feeling and always giving and receiving.

I've been asked by patients why I separate feelings and emotions. Are they not synonymous? Not quite.

A feeling is internal and abstract. It's unrecognizable through our senses. I will never know what you're feeling because it's inside of you. The only way it gets expressed outwardly is through some sort of physical means—whether through words or actions. Emotions are that physical expression.

If the way your boss is squinting at you is similar to how your mother looked when she was angry, you may feel that he's upset with you. But it may be just how he looks when he concentrates. It's the same facial expression, but has been interpreted as two different feelings.

This is why there's so much confusion and debate over who is right and who is wrong in a given situation. Energy can be transformed into anything. If I attach a particular feeling to a certain event, this doesn't mean you will have the same feeling towards it. Who is right and who is wrong? It's your personal perception.

How many times have you been upset with co-workers or employees because of what you thought they meant, not realizing it was a total misunderstanding? These upsetting feelings could have been avoided if you knew what they really meant. But you can't sense their feelings. You can't see, hear, touch or smell them without physical expression. Emotions are exactly that – the physical expression of feelings

Emotions are governed by the Communicator Principle and your Communicator Trait.

We communicate in three ways. The first is verbal language or speech. You need to physically move your vocal chords to produce a sound. The second is body language. This can be hand signals, facial expressions, or stance. Then there is non-body language. This is something outside of you such as a pen and pad, phone, computer, fax, other people, and so on. In any of these three cases you need some type of physical entity to communicate and connect with another person, thing, or event. Therefore, communication is a *connection.*

However, the Communicator is also *disconnection*. If I want to disconnect from you, I would use some or all of the three ways of communicating. I would perhaps say offensive words, wave my hands in a violent way, or send you a nasty message. If you want to find out what the message inside a fortune cookie says, then you need to physically break the cookie to analyze the message that is waiting to be discovered. Hence, the two components of the Communicator are *connection* and *disconnection.*

SUMMARY

Let's quickly review the three principles.

You have learned how the Director Principle, your Director Trait, and your thoughts are the same because each is governed by the Director Principle.

DIRECTOR CHARACTERISTICS

- Direction in Life
- Perception ➡ Belief ➡ Faith ➡ Trust
- Controls and Influences Your Choices
- Organizer/Manager
- Sequencer/Planner
- Regulator of Imbalance
- Gate Keeper of Your Comfort Zone
- Commander

I've summarized a list of characteristics of the Director above. Let's review them. We discussed that the Director controls the direction of our life through our perception, which creates our beliefs. Our beliefs create our faith. Faith is not spiritual but mental since our beliefs reside there. Our faith then creates our trust. It controls and influences our choices, organizes and manages and sequences and plans everything within your life. It regulates any imbalance and creates and determines the size of our comfort zone. It's the commander of our body. It determines our direction.

Remember how you learned in Chapter 16 that you have three traits called the Dominant Trait, Mediator Trait, and Sabotaging Trait? Whichever of the three traits you favor more is your Dominant Trait. The one you least favor is your Sabotaging Trait, the non-dominant trait. The Mediator Trait is the bridge between the two. The order of all three determines your Personality Stress Sequence.

If your Dominant Trait is the Director Trait, you may have instances where you micromanage or give your opinion without being asked. And since your Director Trait represents the Dominant Trait, your Mediator Trait, and Sabotaging Trait are left to be either the Communicator or Supplier Traits. Conversely, if you don't take control, then your Sabotaging Trait is represented by your Director Trait. Your Dominant Trait and Mediator Trait will be represented by the other two traits. Remember, the Mediator Trait is the bridge between the Dominant and Silent Traits. Although not relevant to this book, the role of your Mediator Trait is covered in detail in my online course, at www.dragrios.com/courses.

Next let's review the Supplier Principle, the Supplier Trait, and feelings.

SUPPLIER CHARACTERISTICS

- Supplier of Energy
- Exchange/Transform
- Giver/Rejecter/Releaser
- Taker/Receiver/Attractor
- Fills Voids/Wants/Desires
- Feelings

Your Supplier Trait supplies energy—whether to yourself or to others. Energy is exchanged or transformed by the Supplier Trait, without being created or destroyed. You give or take because of how valuable something or someone is in filling a void in your life. A void is a want or need. A void is your desire.

This is where your feelings are governed. You want your desires to be fulfilled because it *feels good*. Everything you do is to feel good and to avoid the greatest imagined amount of pain—unless pain feels good to you. There is more detail on this subject and how it has affected my chronically ill patients in Chapter 3.

If it seems to you to be more painful to *effectively deal* with your problems than to *ignore* them, however painful it may seem to others, *having problems* will be your metric for understanding what 'feeling good' means.

Your Supplier's job is to fill your voids or desires by transforming or exchanging one thing for another. You supply to others and yourself valuable feelings (energy) so everyone's voids or desires can be fulfilled.

If your Dominant Trait is the Supplier Trait, you may overreact by being too sensitive to criticism. If the Supplier Trait is your Sabotaging Trait, then you may sometimes allow people to take advantage of your kindness. And remember, the mediator is the bridge between the Dominant and Silent Traits.

Finally, let's review the Communicator Principle, the Communicator Trait, and emotions.

COMMUNICATOR CHARACTERISTICS

- Connector/Interactor
- Facilitator/Catalyst
- Transporter/Transmitter/Carrier
- Expresser of Emotions
- Disconnect/Break/Unlink
- Unfold

Nothing can be communicated without some sort of physical entity. We use the three communication methods described above to connect or disconnect. This communication is attached to an expressed emotion.

You may have noticed that I'm communicating to you right now. My words are connecting with you, causing an indirect interaction between us. How well you think I'm connecting or communicating will facilitate or disallow for that interaction. Therefore, the Communicator is the facilitator or catalyst.

The Communicator is also the transporter or transmitter. You transport your supply of feelings to me through physical emotions. This physical emotion can be in the form of words, bodily actions, or mediating physical objects like a cellphone.

Your emotions 'emote' or express your feelings. Hence, the Communicator is an expresser of emotions. This expression either connects or disconnects us from others.

If your Dominant Trait is the Communicator Trait, you may overreact by expressing too much. If the Communicator Trait is your Sabotaging Trait, you may fail to express yourself or completely detach from stressful situations.

In summary, *Life's One Law* is made up of the Principles of the **Director**, **Supplier** and **Communicator** which allow us to use our traits so we can think, feel, and express, respectively. These three basic principles, working simultaneously with each other, make and govern everyone and everything in the universe.

I wanted to end this chapter with a thought for those of you who may still look at life as complex and not simple. You are fully correct to think this way. Complex would not exist if not for simplicity. Simple would not exist because there would be nothing to compare it to.

Consider complex carbohydrates, which are created by connecting simple sugars together. The more you connect, the more complex it can get. The same with the principles.

Start connecting them with each other and life will seem to be complex. The complex carbohydrate can be overwhelming if you did not know the simple sugars. It is like anything else and the principles are no exception.

Going back to the previous diagram on in this chapter, there is a *hidden message* explaining a crucial part of life. If the three principles make-up *Life's One Law*, what creates each principle? The answer - the three principles because within each principle contains the three principles. For instance, the Director Principle is represented by the mobius image which is made up of the three principles.

The Director Principle cannot exist by itself -- all three must work in conjunction with one another. The Director Principle is made up of the Supplier Principle, the Communicator Principle and yes, even itself, the Director Principle, because nothing can exist without these three principles. Just as the organ cannot exist without the cell, the cell cannot exist without its cells and so on. This is infinite. There is no end to it. Life is a puzzle within a puzzle within a puzzle, using the same three pieces over and over again. The three pieces are the principles. The same for the Supplier and Communicator Principles.

To go a little further, the six seasons follow the same pattern. Since the three principles are the six seasons split, you will also find that the six seasons are within each season. Whether you are in summer or relinquis, you will need to make a decision, replenish, detach, plan, give, and connect. This is true for each season.

Everything is interchangeable and depending on how detailed you want to be, you can choose to view each season or each principle (a season is half a principle) with all six seasons or the three principles.

As you have already learned, the principles are interchangeable with our traits. The only difference is the Director Principle becomes the Director Trait, the Supplier Principle becomes the Supplier Trait, and the Communicator

Principle becomes the Communicator Trait. Just like the principles, we all have the three within us.

The traits can be sequenced in different combinations. This is why we seem complex. But we are basically all the same despite our differences. It's still the same three pieces used over and over in different orders.

This is why someone with the same Personality Stress Sequence seems to handle a situation differently than you; it's the same basic sequence, just used to different degrees. This is how we and nature exist and coexist. The three principles make up everyone and everything.

If you'd like to explore this in further detail, please view my program. ***Your Stress Antidote: Get Immediate Relief!*** (www.dragrios.com/courses) is a program which allows you to easily find your Personality Stress Sequence, Sabotaging Trait, and Antidote.

CHAPTER TWENTY

THE SIX SEASONS EQUAL THE THREE PRINCIPLES

I've shown you the six seasons, how they work, and provided exercises you can do to maximize the effect of each season in your life and business. I then reviewed how there were two sides to each of the seasons and whichever side you focused on would give you different types of experience.

I explained that the seasons were created by three principles and that they were just two halves of each of them. I reviewed how these three principles are elements of the one encompassing law called *Life's One Law.*

This chapter will reveal which seasons relate to which principle and how you can utilize this knowledge to increase your business, sales, contacts, income, and personal life.

I shared with you the three words that explain the entire inner-workings of life – director, supplier and communicator -- and I expressed how these words concisely describe three principles that govern it.

Using the diagram from chapter 5, summer and winter are your Director seasons.

Summer denotes power and production, whereas winter has hidden power and potential. These seasons also represent knowledge. Summer experiences it on the outside while winter has wisdom within. Your direction or understanding of what to do is determined by what you've learned from summer and your plan for future summers that you developed in winter.

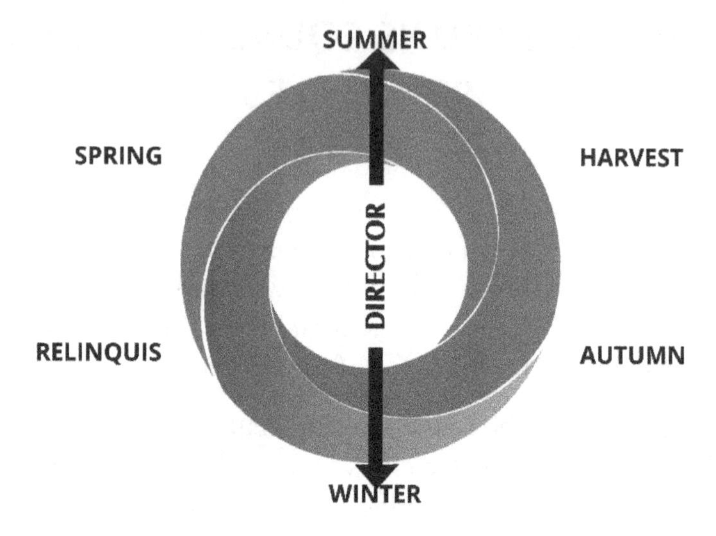

Attention and intention are Director Traits. You place your attention within summer and set your intention in winter. Your intention for a particular goal starts in winter. Once it is achieved during summer, then your attention or concentration is required to keep it steadfast.

Summer is about the quality and quantity of what you produce. The better your produce, the more power and authority you have in the market place, and the more people come to you for your product. This is the follow through, the discipline a business owner or board of directors needs to have to continue to do what is necessary to serve their customers. If your attention wanes, so does your authority, and chaos ensues.

But the role of authority can be misused as well. This is when many people who move into a position of power, like a managerial position, can abuse it. Use this power to inspire, not to destroy people. Use it wisely and with a mind to mutual benefit. Micromanaging is the result of too much attention, which causes as much of an imbalance as no attention.

Winter is the potential for using your talents and energy wisely or foolishly. This is the planning stage, where you obtain the knowledge from your past summer and decide to stay on course or change your direction. Your inner director should be aware of past experience. With trust and faith in yourself and your team, set a course for actualizing your next summer produce. This is your intent.

However, winter can also be misused. Failing to obtain the necessary knowledge to better your product, planning to mislead your employees or customers, or making arbitrary or selfish decisions will take your business on a course toward destruction.

Having no or little purpose in life is based on your intention, whether for your business, a meeting or for any other goal you wish to obtain. If you do not spend enough or if you spend too much time in winter, both can cause a misaim creating anything but the summer you have envisioned.

Perhaps your intended target was not met and you missed your mark. There is no cause for concern because you now know which season to look to create a different intention.

Your summer and winter provide the basis to guide your customers in the direction of buying from you or not. They're looking for you to direct them to your product or to redirect them to your competitors. Being clear and providing precise knowledge of your product and its benefit will direct customers to buy from you.

Once you obtain the knowledge needed to take your business in a different direction or stay on course, you look toward another law to fuel whatever decision you made in summer and winter.

This Supplier Principle creates harvest and relinquis. These seasons provide the desire to put your thoughts (your plan) into action. Without this desire, fate (the seasons) will give you what you are projecting from within. If you take no control to shape your intention then you will receive what unconsciously you're sending out.

LIFE'S ONE LAW

6 SEASONS CYCLE

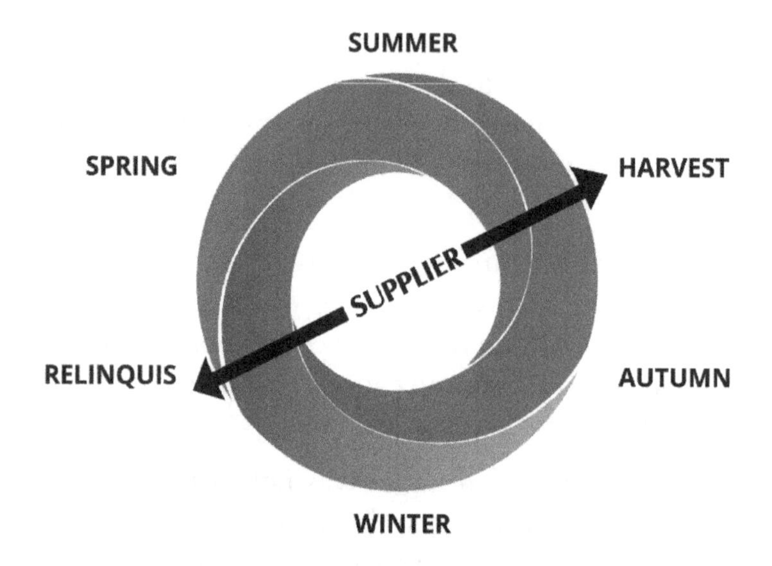

This principle is to find the balance so you can replenish yourself and give to others thereby creating an equal exchange so no one feels slighted.

If you're projecting that you lack money, resources, or customers (because you didn't plan in winter or examine the quality of your fruit in summer), then you'll receive what you are projecting in kind. Lack produces lack. If the sunflower's nectar is not sweet, it won't attract bees to fertilize it. If it could think, it might wonder why all the other flowers were doing so well. It would think its creator has something out for it or that it's done something wrong and is being punished.

Punishment means being disciplined. *Self*-punishment happens when you fail to do what was necessary in summer and winter to obtain knowledge and understanding of the fruit you produced. You were not disciplined enough to stay consistent. Or you didn't have enough faith in yourself to plan in winter -- or maybe you had too much faith in someone else. You received what you put out because of what you did not give to your business or in your life. The Supplier Principle gave you what you felt you deserved.

The Supplier Principle uses the seasons of harvest and relinquis to supply or replenish your feelings and desires. Your thoughts and decisions from the previous seasons are now being fueled to ready yourself for the unleashing of the power that lay dormant within your product or service of summer or of the plan you created in winter. The desire to put your marketing into action or the desire of your customer to receive it, gives you the ability to find a void and fill it.

During harvest you gather your thoughts and feelings, and during relinquis where you give so those thoughts and feelings can be accepted or rejected. This is where you find the value of your time spent in summer and winter. How valuable is your product or service? Will it be accepted by your prospects or rejected? Depending on those results, what feeling will you give or receive? This is where you accept or reject the challenges you face.

The Supplier Principle offers value. You gather and give what you feel is valuable to you, your customers, and employees. If this value is diminished in any way, then the possibility of being rejected increases. If you sell a poorly made product that you wouldn't use yourself, then you're going to have a tough time convincing others to use it.

Autumn and spring are the two halves of the Communicator Principle. Autumn disconnects to eliminate what is no longer needed. Spring is when connection is paramount to build anew.

You can have a clear and concise plan, a valuable product or service and the burning desire to share it with others, but if you fail to communicate the benefit of your product effectively, then your director and supplier are helpless.

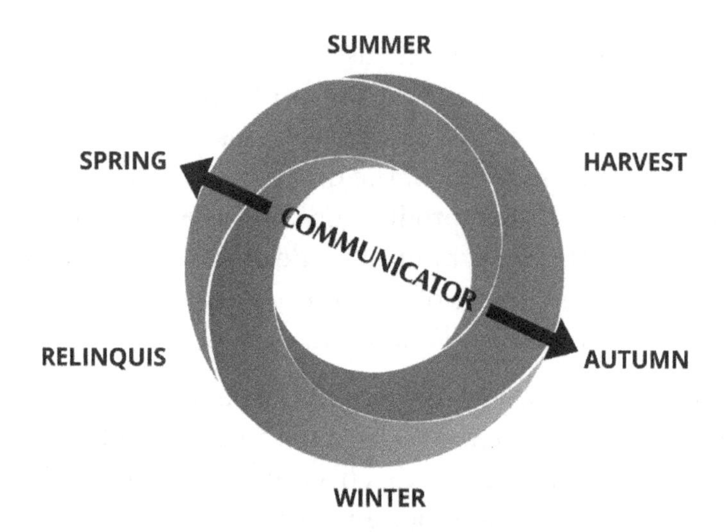

How effective is your pitch, your marketing, and PR department? Do you communicate clearly how your product and service can benefit your client's needs? How about your return policy? Your policy for the dismissal of employees? When you give projects to your staff, do you communicate without causing confusion?

The Communicator Principle solidifies the deal or causes it to fall apart.

Just as you need all six seasons, you need all three principles. The six seasons and the three principles are the same. All are parts of the whole called *Life's One Law*.

Examples Of *Life's One Law*

Let's say you need to go to the airport to catch a flight to an important meeting. A limousine driver picks you up bright and early. But he didn't use the seasons too well, wasn't prepared, and needs to refuel. You're understandably not happy.

The driver in this scenario represents the Director. He's in charge of steering the limousine and will determine which direction the limousine will go. The gasoline is the Supplier. It's the fuel running the limousine. The limousine is the Communicator because it's what's used by the driver to move from one place to another, connecting or transporting you from your house to the airport. It's a simple example which shows that for anything to occur in life you need all three principles working simultaneously with each other.

What happens if the gas station runs out of gas and there's no more in the tank? The driver is still there, you're still in the limousine, but with no gas to run it, will you still get to the airport? What happens if the limousine has a full tank of gas, but the driver walks off the job? Or if you overslept and the driver leaves without picking you up?

You need all three to get to the airport—the driver (Director), gasoline (Supplier), and the limousine (Communicator). Remove one and nothing happens.

Another example is the way our bodies work. The brain is the Director. Food, which is energy for the body, is the Supplier. The muscles, when they contract, move us from one place to the other—our Communicator. Not one of these things can be removed without immobilizing or killing us.

How about a company? The manager is the Director, the product the company sells is the Supply, and employees are the Communicator. Managers would no longer be managers if they had no employees to manage. But without a manager to orchestrate the employees to work in harmoniously with one another, there would be chaos and no work would get done.

And of course, if there is no product, then there's no need for the other two to even exist.

Let's do a quick review of the three principles.

- Summer and winter are the two halves of the Director Principle governing the Director Trait which is your thoughts.
- Harvest and relinquis are the two halves of the Supplier Principle governing the Supplier Trait which is your feelings.
- Autumn and spring are the two halves of the Communicator Principle governing the Communication Trait which is your emotions.

Everything exists because of these three principles. Everything that you see, hear, feel, touch and taste are all three principles happening at the same time. You, your company and your employees are all the three principles interacting with each other, at the same time.

With the power of *Life's One Law* you can implement and affect change in your thoughts, feelings, and emotions at any time and during any season. It's a shortcut to getting exactly what you want and need for success.

In the next chapter, I will explain how you can quickly get on track with any project or relationship by focusing on just your Sabotaging Trait.

CHAPTER TWENTY-ONE

YOUR COMPANY HAS A SABOTAGING TRAIT

The Sabotaging Trait is responsible for balancing our energy and lessening our resistance in every aspect of our life. We can utilize this tool that lies within to understand and deal with everyday worries. Here life's solutions become evident.

We know that for every solution, there is a problem. The opposite is true as well. The Sabotaging Trait brings you your problems and challenges along with a solution (the Antidote). It's your starting point to direct yourself along the path to more or less resistance.

Less, but not *no* resistance. We want simple, but we don't want easy. We want challenges to continue to inspire us. We want to evolve and expand our experiences. It's the Sabotaging Trait that challenges us and brings us contrast, resistance for us not to be bored and to focus on evolving. The Antidote decreases confusion, impatience, and inaction so we can focus on that expansion and not on the resistance. Remember, they are both there at the same time. Where will your focus lie?

The Antidote is ready and waiting to be used to maximize your ability for whatever tasks lie ahead.

Imagine knowing exactly what derails you from achieving your vision—in life or business. Uncovering your Sabotaging Trait and Antidote will allow you to fully understand why life and your business are redirecting you on a path that you didn't plan to follow.

From there, you will see why your business isn't doing well, or why certain things that did work in the past are no longer working. This can make or break a company.

Whether dealing with the inner workings of your business or your life, your Sabotaging Trait is always there waiting for instructions to respond with trust or fear.

Your Sabotaging Trait puts a name and a meaning to your fear. The inability to place your finger on what is really fueling your fear creates more fear. Uncovering your Antidote gives you that knowledge and understanding which in turns neutralizes the fear. If you know what is causing it, then you know how to counteract it.

Remember, when I use the word *fear*, this is anything that makes you feel uncomfortable, no matter the degree. This is on either end of the scale that I discussed in Chapter 9. This can be anything from making a cold call to a new sales prospect to walking into your boss' office after you've made a costly mistake. The Antidote gives you the action step needed to make that call or confront your boss – and also understand why you made that mistake in the first place.

Time and time again, once my patients understood the driving force behind their fear, they could immediately neutralize it or start on a path to correcting it. It brought out the trust within themselves to have the courage to move forward.

Of course, as soon as they stopped using it, they would revert to the old pattern or habit. However, they knew when they were ready to alter course, they had the solution to do it immediately.

You use your Sabotaging Trait instead of your Antidote most times because it is more comfortable to do so. The goal for my patients was to get them to always be more comfortable using the Antidote than the Sabotaging Trait.

I first discovered that **a company had a Personality Stress Sequence** when I looked at my relationship with my practice.

I wondered why I couldn't keep my business consistent. Why I couldn't seem to avoid the ups and downs. One day, sitting in my office, I realized that the business was *responding* to how I was or wasn't implementing certain aspects of it. How I felt and thought one day would create a different response on another. My practice was taking on a human characteristic and responding in the same way as a person would.

What was happening was that my *personal* Sabotaging Trait and my *practice's* Sabotaging Trait were in conflict with one another. Both Sabotaging Traits were feeding each other.

My practice's communication, marketing materials, social media blogging and in-office conversations regarding treatment (The Communicator Principle) was not being consistently implemented by *my* Sabotaging Trait (The Director Principle).

I was always focusing on the *Dominant Trait of the practice* (Supplier). I focused too heavily on the value of my treatment programs, failing to realize that by not focusing on the communication aspect of the practice, I could never give my patients the full value of my service.

When I figured out the Sabotaging Trait and Antidote of my practice and how it was interacting with my personal Sabotaging Trait and Antidote, my practice stayed consistently busy. I didn't need to constantly work on the treatment, service, and products I was giving patients. That had already been developed the best they could be at that time. It was the business' communication which needed work. Applying the business' Antidote quickly effected the needed change and I stopped being the best kept secret in town.

Now let's look at some characteristics that a Sabotaging Trait may have.

Each principle takes on the characteristics of each trait. For example, maybe your Dominant Trait is a strong communicator, but your Sabotaging Trait lacks consistency and self-control. If you do not control your over-communication with the customer, then this is likely where, in the past you literally talked yourself out of a sale. You overwhelmed them by giving them too much information. They left looking for something less overwhelming. Your product may be better than your competitor's, but because you didn't communicate it clearly, you lost the sale.

Knowing this in advance will stop you in the future. Imagine knowing your Personality Stress Sequence and understanding how you can duplicate that sale every time. Imagine your employees and your managers knowing your company's Sabotaging Trait and Antidote. Imagine knowing your employees' Sabotaging Trait and Antidote so you can support them in the way *they need* to be supported and NOT in the way *you think* they need to be supported. (This is what I can provide in a workshop or online courses. Please visit www.dragrios.com for more information.)

I want to give you a little glimpse into the three possible Sabotaging Traits.

The Director Saboteur

If your Sabotaging Trait followed the Director Principle, it would be called a Director Saboteur. Of course, a saboteur is one who engages in sabotage; this is what this part of you does. It can manifest as either end of the director spectrum where you can either sabotage yourself by becoming unaware and inconsistent or move to the other side and become completely hyper-focused. Just as the Seasonal Bar Graph shows (see Chapter 15), there are different degrees of these behaviors.

If the Director is your Sabotaging Trait, you typically don't follow through because you are indecisive or unclear on what to do. You are indecisive because you don't have faith in yourself. Director Saboteurs are scattered, disorganized, and hate to follow through on tasks.

Conversely, a Director Saboteur can also be laser-focused. You can lose track of time and ignore other tasks or people who are more important. For instance, you may work at night or go on social media instead of spending time with your family.

By incorporating the tools I specifically discovered for the Director, you become less overwhelmed and more in control. You become more organized and your life will be manageable. People will trust you again because they know the job will get done. This is how a Director Saboteur balances out life.

The Supplier Saboteur

Supplier Saboteurs, likewise can run to either extreme. The over-suppliers are typically overly sensitive, or feel unworthy or undeserving. You are too patient and tolerant with people to the point where others treat you like a doormat. You take on too much because you cannot say no. Feeling unworthy causes you to be afraid of rejection.

However, if your Supplier Saboteurs is an under-supplier, you may have been told you are self-absorbed. This may be because you automatically go into a protective mode to hold on to what little you have left. Being self-absorbed, intolerant, and impatient are the other sides of you. You reject others before they reject you. You may feel those people aren't worthy of your company or your valuable assets.

Once you use the tools of the Supplier, you will have self-love. You won't be tolerant of being mistreated. Your desires will then be more easily supplied to you. This is where the Supplier finds balance.

The Communicator Saboteur

Communicator Saboteurs are distant, quiet, and non-confrontational. You're a listener, not a talker. You like to be in the background instead of the limelight. You express or communicate infrequently. You degrade yourself if you make a visible mistake. This can discourage you from communicating your thoughts and feelings with others.

On the other side of the spectrum, being a Communicator Saboteur may cause you to over-express yourself or over communicate when you reach your breaking point. This type of break forces you to finally disconnect from your fears and let it all go by saying offensive words or expressing yourself in ways you rarely do. This can often cause more harm than good.

The tools of the Communicator will encourage you to communicate in a more effective way. You'll feel confident, admire your accomplishments, and honor your thoughts. If you don't, others won't. These tools allow you to respect yourself enough to confront their abuse and disconnect from it in a more balanced way.

Your Other Antidotes

Once you focus on the Antidote of the Sabotaging Trait, the Behavioral Domino Effect of success starts. You start to use this more often and subconsciously, then you will create opportunities that will require other Antidotes that I cover in my other courses. The uncovering of your other Antidotes becomes clear and simple as well as powerful and effective.

Life is only made up of three principles and we are no exception. These principles are your three traits and it is how they are placed in your Personality Stress Sequence that will determine whether or not you succeed.

CHAPTER TWENTY-TWO

WHAT WOULD YOU DO WITH A ROTTEN TOMATO?

This is a question I like to ask my patients. Many say they would throw a rotten tomato away. I then ask what they would do if they were a farmer. All of them say they would plant it. Planting the seeds and using the rest of the tomato as fertilizer will give you an abundance of tomatoes in the future.

Seeing the rotten tomato, your rotten problem, as a gift and not a detriment provides the possibility that something good may come out of it.

Your Sabotaging Trait, your cycle of the seasons, can define or sideline you.

You need to focus on you and not the external people, things, and events around you. Notice what you can control. You have the power to change yourself.

This is your chance, your time to change the perception of how you came to be here in this moment. No more blaming you, no more blaming others. Just be grateful for the people, things, and events that you have attracted in your life. Each made you the person you are today.

You are in charge. You decide if you're going to wake up every morning to a blank canvas. You decide what colors you're going to paint with and what scene you're going to paint.

Are you going to use dark and dreary colors or bright and cheery ones? Every day, every hour, every second, you have the ability to change the canvas and start anew.

I would like to convey what I feel are the three basic attributes every business should have: Service, Discernment and Commitment.

Service

The Supplier Principle – Harvest/Relinquis

How can this world be a better place with me in it? How may I serve to guide someone to improve their lives and the people around them? If that customer was me, how would I treat them and would I serve their needs or my wallet?

Why are you here? What's your service to the world? Why do you get up in the morning? Are you excited to start the day? Or can you not wait for bedtime again?

These are service questions. How will you to give to others in order to self-nourish? No one wins when service is a one-way street. Whatever you give, you get in some form or another.

You must give in order to receive. You must give up something first to create a void within you so that something else can occupy that space that you and you alone have created.

However, if you do not replenish yourself in harvest, then so you have nothing or little to give. If you do not have the desire to give, it may be because somewhere you feel your service is not worth giving to others and especially not being paid for it.

This is why self-worth correlates with how successful you are in business and in life. Without it, your service will be worth very little to you and to others. This is when your need for approval comes into place and you can overly give your service away.

Finding that burning desire to provide creates a hole that needs to be filled. Don't look outside of *you* to serve, serve that desire and the people will follow. As I stated previously, it's not what's in it for you only. It's finding out what your desire is and by focusing on that alone, you serve others and yourself fully instantaneously. You cannot focus on the end goal if you are focusing on your desire to serve in the capacity you love. This detaches you from the outcome, the goal that you set.

The tree nourishes itself and its surrounding instantaneously without wanting more for itself or more for others. It is that balanced reciprocity I have talked about. If not, there will be no tree to nourish others in the coming years due to the imbalance. It knows it is intertwined with nature and does not stand alone.

This is the concept that everything is you. We are all interconnected as one, governed by *Life's One Law*. Whatever you do to yourself, you do to others and vice versa. *"As above, so below: as below, so above."*

Approach your service in business in this way and it will transform into the business that everyone will want to experience and be a part of. The main reason people buy from you is because they trust and like you. However, if you don't trust and like yourself, then that's where you need to start first.

This goes for your personal life as well. How are you serving your family? Are they also reciprocating and serving you? How about your friends? Are they leeches who drain the life out of you and never give anything in return? An imbalance in any aspect of life is due to an imbalance of serving.

Are you serving or giving and expecting something in return or by just serving, do you know you will be served in other aspects of your life? The imbalance comes when you refuse others' service because you don't want to be a bother. You do not realize you are stopping not only their gifts to you, but the ability of that person to give.

If you're not giving the service you know you can give, then you're not valuing it properly. Maybe you don't value the product you're selling. It could be that you do not value your ability to serve. Or you're over-serving others and not getting back the energy or the desire you need to continue.

Take a deep, honest look at this concept and find the value and worthiness of your service. Are you rejecting it or are others? How deserving are you of the rewards of your service?

Once you determine this, repeat after me: "**My service is valuable and I accept the abundance I receive.**"

Discernment

The Director Principle – Summer/Winter

According to Merriam-Webster, discernment is "The quality of being able to grasp and comprehend what is obscure." Discernment takes something vague and places a definitive meaning to it.

This is the balance of summer and winter. To view what you produced in your summer and comprehend that the fruit did not cause it to be bitter, but the obscurity of winter that is the true cause.

The inner thoughts of winter produce your outer world of summer. This powerful comprehension allows you to truly take charge and change directions. Discernment causes prudence and judiciousness.

Prudence is "the ability to govern and discipline oneself by the use of reason." Judgment is "the process of forming an opinion or evaluation by discerning and comparing."

This is why you should think before taking an action, to become aware by comparing your options with reason. You can fear this or you can respect it. Ask yourself this important question: *Does this decision best serve my clients and my core values or am I deciding based on fear and ignorance?*

If you do not like what you see in your outer world, then don't use the same world to correct it, but look to the source, your belief system, and how you have directed your choices to create what you see.

Check your belief system if you're not receiving what you want. The disconnect comes when you get upset because the universe didn't give you what you wanted. The disconnect is that this is what you truly believe deep within you.

This is like changing the fruit on the tree instead of changing the plan of winter. As I asked previously, if you had bitter fruit, would you inject the fruit with sugar and then try to pass it off as the real thing?

The problem isn't the fruit, but the preparation. Your beliefs are manifested from within you, but many people have been taught to blame the elements. To blame everything on the outside, not to take the responsibility and say, "It is my knowledge or lack of knowledge as a farmer of life. I would need to have been schooled differently to create a better and more valuable yield."

It comes down to how you judge the people, things and events in your life. If you judge harshly, then you will experience life just as harshly.

Let's say you're at a business networking event and you see someone you can't stand. You instantly feel disdain. Who gets the first dose of this negative energy? You do, since it's coming from you first. Who get the strongest dose? You do, since you feel the despising effect of this person's presence.

But if you feel a lot of joy when you see someone you like and admire? You get the first and strongest dose.

By judging someone, you are immediately judged. If you love, you are loved. What you sow is what you reap. That action is equally and instantaneously returned to you.

If you believe you live in a dog-eat-dog world, then congratulations on the life you've co-created. If you believe in harmony and righteousness in your thoughts and actions, then congratulations on that manifestation as well.

The universe doesn't take ignorance into consideration or as an excuse. If you didn't plan well in winter, you'll get the result of that plan in summer regardless. Some way or another, you will be guided to evolve or dissolve.

To evolve you must dissolve and to dissolve you must evolve. They happen instantaneously. On which will you place your focus and energy?

Become aware that YOU are not taking the action needed to create what you want due to your present knowledge and understanding of the situation. It is not luck, or your Higher Power, waking up one day and saying, "I am in a really bad mood, let me mess with the person reading this book." No, you wake up and say, "Let me not take a different course of action to reap a different yield." This can be based on your unwillingness to do what is necessary for change. Or you are doing what you *think* or *believe* you need, but it isn't the correct course of action for that change.

Discernment is finding truth in your produce (your end result) and changing when it's required.

The Director Principle teaches us to become aware and disciplined. The director is the sensor. Whether you choose to be blind, deaf, and dumb to the results you've sown is up to you.

If this is the case, then repeat after me:

"By becoming aware and disciplined in the implementation of my new beliefs, I am able to focus on the true source of the effects in my life."

Commitment

The Communicator Principle – Autumn/Spring

Your commitment to your beliefs and the unconditional service to the relationships you have created encourages you to preserve and nourish them. These are your partners, clients, employees, and the relationships in your personal life.

The loyalty of their continual support to buy from you creates a bond that is steadfast. This mutual respect solidifies the relationship.

No courage is needed in that relationship, only encouragement and subtle changes to meet the needs of your customers. Your inability to adapt to those small changes can slowly deteriorate a relationship, depending on where your degree of commitment lies.

Adaptation is the true meaning of autumn and spring. This is where change occurs, the building or destruction of bonds that have held together the relationship. If you have trouble with change, then this is where your business will falter. Letting go of the old to make room for the new is the blueprint of nature. An inability to adapt or change will cause rebellion. The rebellion starts within you and the effect is your customer leaving for someone who is more adapted to the times.

Rebellion is confrontation to force a change. This is when you might have been a rebellious teenager. I call it teenage-itis. What are the changes that are happening with family and friends? What relationships are you building or tearing down since they no longer work for you? If you are in a dysfunctional family that will not change and they are forcing you to change against your will, then you need to take a closer look of the fear that is binding you to them.

The same is true with business. Courage and fortitude must be used to oppose your customer's needs or change the way you do business. Are your core values being challenged? Do they need to be changed because they are no longer working? Your core values of honesty and integrity may be confronted by someone who wants you to do something illegal. Do you have the courage to say no?

Likewise, have *you* not been fully honest in your dealings with customers? Are they confronting you? Do you have the courage to *listen*?

Do you feel your world is falling apart? Or is it falling together and your reluctance to let go of people, things, and events in your business and life holding you back from achieving what you really want?

Do you have the courage to fire people who aren't allowing your business to grow and serve? Do you have the courage to fire your habits that are not conducive to an efficient, friendly and fun working atmosphere? Do you have the courage to hire more committed employees? Both firing and hiring require courage and loyalty, reinforcing the bonds you have with your customers.

Confronting your boundaries and expanding your comfort zone shows you that your fear is a self-deception. It's an illusion with only as much power as you're willing to give it.

Your involvement is your choice. You can wait for fate to make those changes. Spring and autumn will come, though. That much is inevitable. Change is constant, with or without you.

Change "worry" to "concern." Worry is essentially praying for something bad to happen. Concern is knowing the consequences and having the fortitude to continue pursuing your vision.

If you have trouble with commitment and change, then repeat after me:

"My willingness to change reinforces my commitment to detach from what is no longer working for me and connect to my true source of inner power."

Now let's put it all together so you can start applying the three principles and the six seasons in a way to create the business and life you desire.

SECTION 4 SUMMARY

- *Life's One Law* is made up of three principles or traits that govern our behavior. This is discovered by delving deeper into Nature's Blueprint.
- The opposite seasons are halves of each trait or principle that work interdependently with the other principles.
- By working on one season, you effect that trait and subsequently all the other traits at the same time. Therefore, you can start changing your behavior and the results you create by focusing on just one trait.
- Your Sabotaging Trait is the one that is causing your conflicts or challenges in your life and business so that you can evolve with truth or dissolve through fear. As you use its Antidote, then you can stabile yourself in the True Season of balance.
- Service, Discernment and Commitment allow you to apply each principle in a balanced way without really getting too involved in the process. Here you can achieve peace and harmony by focusing on the one that may be challenging for you. This allows balance to automatically enter your business and life so you can start achieving the results you so desire.

SECTION 5: APPLY THE TEACHINGS OF THIS BOOK

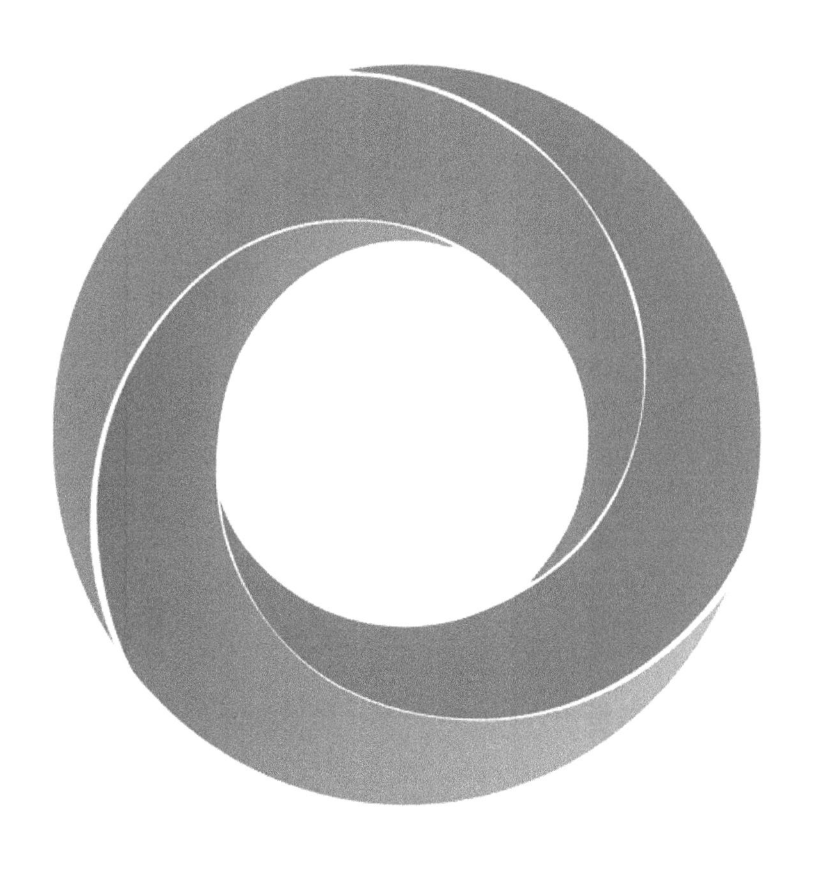

CHAPTER TWENTY-THREE

Now Apply It

Obviously one of the reasons for reading this book is to increase your success. When I ask people for their meaning of success, I receive many different answers. Some may consider success as some sort of achievement. Others may equate success with the accumulation of wealth, or high status, or attaining a position of authority.

If we take these definitions of success and look at the cycle of the seasons, then the seasons produce success every time. Remember I said earlier, it depends on how you view success and anything else for that matter. If you were unsuccessful at being rich, you were successful at being poor.

The same goes for the seasons. If you created an outcome that you did not desire, then you used the Fear Seasons or you used the True Seasons and created exactly what you *needed*, even though you may not agree.

How many times have you received something you thought was the worst thing ever and it turned out to be the best thing that could have happened? Once you changed your perception about it or obtained new information, things switched.

Either way, nature gave you a blueprint you have unknowingly always followed and now the veil has been lifted. You can now have a greater understanding of what will happen depending on the season you are in, how you work it and how accepting you are of the next one.

You need to remember that if you are focusing on one of the seasons, you should look for its counterpart because it's there, in the background, working just as hard. Nature is always looking to balance. If there is resistance on your part, you may win in the beginning, but you are not going to get your way in the end unless you dance with nature instead of fighting against it.

You now have the dance steps. All you have to do is practice. Forget the old dance and start practicing the new one. You want to get to the point where the new dance is more comfortable than the old one -- to the point that the old dance is unbearable. That's when you break a habit.

What To Do First

Taking a chance without thinking it through, finding the knowledge to go from a risky move to a calculated one or going on your gut feeling, may not always work. In this book, I have laid out exercises for you to determine which season you are in, for your business and your life.

Start with summer because this is your end result. This gives you your knowledge of what happened. By starting here, you use the Director Principle (summer and winter) and determine where your Director has taken you, which direction you are facing and whether you still want to travel in this direction. To look at it another way, where are you now in your business and your personal life? Are you happy, miserable, or indifferent? What has happened in the past that has brought you to this point? What are your beliefs, your daily thoughts and do you have faith and trust in yourself?

Once you determine your direction, look to the Supplier Principle (harvest and relinquis). Do you have a burning desire to follow the path you have laid before yourself? Do you devalue yourself and others daily or are you going through life numbing yourself? How valuable is your product and service and would you buy it? Do you value your life? Have you given enough to yourself and are you giving to others to keep the flow of supply going on both ends? Any blockage on either end causes a decrease or stoppage of flow to all parties?

Lastly, by using the Communicator Principle (autumn and spring), you can determine if your actions match or contradict your words. You can have all the greatest thoughts and burning desires, but if they do not match your actions, then you create a powerful resistance – turmoil and suffering.

Are you a good communicator? Are you able to confront the problem at hand immediately or do you need enough pain to finally take action? Do you encourage yourself or have you surrounded yourself with people who discourage you and keep you in their misery?

By using all three principles in your business and personal life, you can get an idea of where you stand, how you feel about it and your willingness to act to stay put or change directions.

What To Do Next

Give yourself and others a break. This is so important! If you are not able to forgive and be grateful to yourself and others for the events that have occurred, then you cannot release yourself from the chains of the past. It will be impossible to live in the present moment. The same goes by living in fear of the future. Will you serve the past, present or future? You cannot serve more than one master. In other words, you cannot focus on more than one thing at a time.

I try to emphasize this to my patients and my business clientele. If you and I wanted to visit you when you were 10 years old, can we do that? No. Only you can visualize that in your mind because the past is stored there. So, the past is an illusion.

For example, if after reading this chapter, you plan on going to the grocery store but your significant other stops you and takes you out to lunch, was your future real or something in your head? Again, your future is but a mere illusion.

However, if you catastrophize about the past or the future, by just focusing on either one and being upset about it, you leave your present and make them your present state.

I would tell my patients, especially my autoimmune patients, that by reacting to the past or future, their body would think danger was actually present. It would then take action and protect itself. Cortisol levels would increase, blood would rush to the brain and muscles preparing for fight or flight along with a whole slew of other actions readying the body for war.

The sheer thought of this caused their feelings to fuel their worry, producing a reaction of protection with a rush of hormones that aggravated their condition with inflammation and destruction. And all of this based on an illusion.

I am not going to get into the physics aspect that the past, present and future are happening simultaneously. However, I will note that they all play a part in your life and how you utilize them determines if they will be for your benefit or your detriment.

By releasing yourself from these illusions, then you will be ready to fully embrace the seasonal exercises.

Lastly

Once you have ascertained your position, have released yourself from the bondage of the past, present and future, you are ready to start taking care of you. It is not a selfish act but an essential one.

If the tree does not stop the supply to its outside world of leaves and regroup, it will not last the winter. Give yourself permission to give to you, take the time necessary to revamp your business and your life, if necessary, and follow all of the seasonal exercises I have laid out in this book.

Remember, as the book that attracts dust on the bookshelf and the content within it is never used, then so too will you attract a protective layer and over time, will be forgotten and covered.

If you feel this book is of value, then read it a few times, mark it up with notes and devour it so it can be a part of you. If you feel it is not, then pass it to someone else so they may benefit.

CHAPTER TWENTY-FOUR

TAPPING INTO ABUNDANCE

Do you believe in unlimited or limited abundance? Your answer will determine what you see in your outside world.

However, merely believing in unlimited abundance does not guarantee you will experience it. Your winter, or the inner knowing or that belief that gives you a sense that things will work out, is great but if it is not fueled by a burning desire (relinquis), then nothing gets manifested. Instead of moving into spring, you access its counterpart, autumn, causing a disconnect. It's a crossing of the bridge that links spring and autumn allowing you to bypass summer and harvest. (See diagram below.

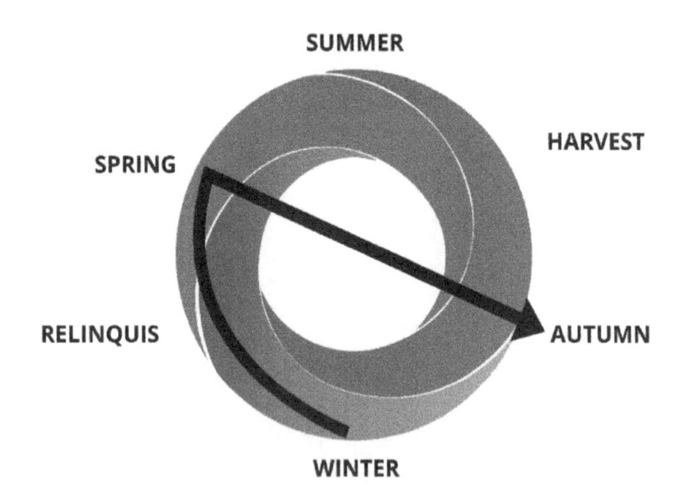

The same goes for the other seasons. Depending on where you are at on the circle, if you cannot go into the next season, its opposite will take over and you will find yourself back tracking. But it isn't back tracking but a forward movement to a "Let's try this again." By being cognizant of this, your mind can perceive this differently.

The rational mind is summer because it believes only in what it can see, hear, smell, touch and taste. It only senses the fruit, the limited produce that the tree generated. There is a limitation in summer. This is where your limited beliefs are and to find the unlimited supply, you need to look in winter. The creative and unlimited mind is also in winter where all our potentialities lay.

Winter is your unlimited ideas, infinite solutions and the boundless abundance that awaits you. Winter is where there are no limitations. Summer is the limiting season in which you assume what you sense is all that there is.

You may want more customers, more money, more time. These are all the potentialities that await you. The ice sits there waiting to melt to release the life-giving water within. Similarly, your abundance within you waits for you to have the burning desire to awaken the giant within.

By going into winter, you must first ask yourself, since winter is clarity, do you believe in infinite abundance? Do you believe that you are deserving of that abundance? Do you have a way to serve people that will give you the ability to receive the type of abundance that you desire? If any one of those answers are a no, then resistance occurs, blocking the flow of abundance into your life.

Follow the True Seasons to make them a yes. With a no, you cause resistance, struggle and pain. If you can't find it, I would be honored to guide you through it.

Once you can do this, there is nothing to find. It is already around you. Be clear in what you want in your business and your life, have the burning desire to do it (which needs to be fun) and determine in what way will you serve others. If you do not know how you can serve, no worries. Just be clear with the desire to serve and it will find you. Be consistent in thought and desire -- and not for merely a few seconds or a few hours but for days, months and years.

Are you serving with love and true giving or with disdain and false giving? Remember, relinquis and harvest happen at the same time. So, what you give out, you get back.

This is like the earth -- when it is in harvest in the Northern Hemisphere, relinquis is equally giving in the Southern Hemisphere. The same happens with you. It is an impossibility for you to give without receiving. The universe demands balance.

If you jump into a pool and create a hole in the water, does the hole remain? No. The water fills it up. If you dig a hole, the hole remains but you created an equal mound of dirt. You cannot get away from balance, a state of equilibrium.

This is the reason why by focusing on how you can be of service and what void you can fill, you will summon the universe to give equally to you.

Yes, at times you may see a new customer come out of "nowhere" and other times you may not see the physical evidence of your service. It is the latter that is determining if you are doing it out of truth/love or out of fear. It you are serving others because you need money, then you will receive the harvest of fear. If you are serving others out of love, then your harvest will be love – your truth.

Is your service based on doing for others or for yourself? Are you giving this service or your product to people out of how it can change their lives or how you expect it will change yours? Right there is the determination of your immediate harvest, your abundance, your replenishment.

In what ways can you be a value to others? Are you focusing on *how* you are doing all of this and forgetting *why* you are doing this?

Spring is your action.

You may hear that your vibration is very important. What is vibration? It is the expansion and contraction of energy. Expansion and contraction is also growth and protection, high and low, sending out and bringing in, giving and receiving. It doesn't matter what you call it because those are just words, but it is what you feel from it that matters. Your feeling determines the flow in which people, things and events come into and out of your life.

Again, it is not only about feelings. It is about clarity, feeling and how you serve, which is the action in which all the first two get manifested.

What is the motivation behind your asking for the desires you want manifested in your business and life? Are you serving because you are inspiring or are you asking because you are expiring?

Any Fear Season will block or increase your resistance to the flow of the unlimited abundance that is all around you. Will you allow or disallow because of your burning desire to get instead of the need to give? However, if you give too much it still causes an imbalance, an unfair exchange.

For some, the problem comes because they don't believe that this flow exists. They believe the world is limited and that others much fortunate than themselves have taken most of the pie. What is left for them are the crumbs. If you have this thinking -- that the world is limited -- and you aren't open to thinking differently, then close this book and I wish you all the best.

This limited thinking has caused you to have limited funds, love, or whatever it is you desire. Your outside world is a measuring stick of what you believe, feel and emote on a daily basis. It is a mirror image of your beliefs, your desire and your commitment to others.

Are you ever worried that you need to seek oxygen? No. You know it is all around you unless you enclose yourself in a box. Your potentiality is all around and within you but because you have not taken your mind out of the limited box of thinking, you gasp for survival every day.

Get out of the box! Get out of Fear Summer and move into True Winter and envision what you want your True Summer to be like. Find what you would love to do, your burning desire to serve others and then start serving. Your winter, relinquis and spring will be stimulated -- causing your summer, harvest and autumn to allow you to receive what you want, to disconnect from the life that you no longer want and connect to the one you do.

This is not a fairy tale. It is how the world works. If you want to fight it, then enjoy the abundance of worry, fear and anxiety. If you look at that tree outside of your window and if you feel your potential or destiny is any less than that tree, then I feel for you and the world that you have allowed to continue.

But as soon as you knock, seek and ask as it pertains to the evolution of others, then it will be opened, found and given to you in ways you could only dream of.

Is your service coming from inspiration or desperation? Do you feel empowered or disempowered? Do you feel worthy or unworthy?

I have noticed something the universe does that's interesting once you want to shift your path. It brings a person, thing or event in your life that is opposite to what your new thought is to make sure you truly want it. "Are you sure you want this new desire because you love being a victim. You love misery and complaining. You love the chaos you have all around you."

You *must* say these words. **"This old way no longer serves me; this new thought serves me!"** Then a little bit will go by, maybe a day or two and another event comes in, the usual garbage that you love so much. The universe asks again, "Are you sure you want this new desire because you love being a victim. You love misery and complaining. You love the chaos you have all around you."

Again, you must answer, ***"This no longer serves me; this new thought serves me!"***

It may do this again and the more you say those words, your vibration changes from the old to the new. The universe MUST give you what you desire because you will now attract the people, things and events into your life to match your new vibration. **It is law! *Life's One Law*!**

Your gratitude of relinquis gives you the appreciation of harvest. Are you focused on gratitude and appreciation or focused on ingratitude and depreciation of what you have received and allowed?

By not being grateful, the opposite must come to you, a depreciation of your worth and if you feel you are not worth anything, then why would any abundance come to you?

There is nothing you do not have. Everything is inside of you. All your potential is waiting to be manifested in physical form. The tree is anchored into the ground by its roots along with the soil where all the nutrients lie, all the potentiality to continue to flourish is there waiting for it to tap into it.

You can't see where you are tapped into because it is not visible. Some may see it, feel it or experience it. It is there. Science does not have the tools yet to prove it, but just look around and within the ocean, nature's blueprint is feeding and evolving life and everything that is within it.

As I said before, believe that what you want is already here. Take your stance that this is what you desire and have the trust and faith in winter that it is yours. Do not base your trust and faith on your past experiences but in the present state of your being. Only the present exists and the past and future only exist in your mind and they are illusions.

Know that your clarity and burning desire will manifest what you envision.

LIFE'S ONE LAW

Life's One Law is nature's blueprint and in this book I have shown you some of the effects it can have on your business and life. This book is intended to be an introduction to how life really works. Remember, this is only the tip of the iceberg of what I have discovered.

The Personality Stress Sequence gave you the three traits, which are your Dominant Trait, Mediator Trait, and Sabotaging Trait. Depending on how the three principles took on the characteristic of each trait shows you why you handled stressful situations the way you did and will continue to do in the future.

I explained that your Sabotaging Trait starts the Behavioral Domino Effect leading to desperation. Its opposite, the Antidote, forces you to shift that effect to a feeling of inspiration.

I gave you exercises you can use to understand how the seasons are affecting every aspect of your business and your life. You were also given three words to focus on to strengthen your business and life and start finding that key to success. They were service, discernment, and commitment.

I also discussed how these seasons can be used to cause your business and life to turn around or remain consistent. Once you can see the gift in adversity, you can start using your intention to create what you really want.

If you aren't making the money you want, the business you want, the life you want, or you have those but are now overwhelmed, then *Life's One Law* is unbalanced. If you don't correct this imbalance, it will correct itself and you may not like the results.

Life is not complicated. It is our thoughts, feelings and emotions that complicate it. Once you understand how *Life's One Law* works through you, then you can fully embrace all the universe has intended to give you. You can rub your hands like I do and say, "I wonder what gift I'm getting!"

If you lower your resistance by using your Antidote and allow it to guide you, there is nothing you cannot imagine and strive to achieve.

Life was not meant to kill you, but challenge you so that you can experience it fully.

Remember your business and personal life are not separate but are guided by you. By focusing on the effects of the outside world and never looking at the source that created it (*YOU*), you will wonder why nothing seems to change.

But by looking at your summer produce, the tree of knowledge, you can gather the information needed to change it. Once you have a solid plan and have the burning desire to put it into action, then and only then will your results change. And you'll discover you had the power all along.

That power is directed, supplied, and communicated to you through only one law—***Life's One Law!***

SECTION 5 SUMMARY

- Knowledge is NOT power but potential power waiting to be acted upon. Yes, I gave you a lot of information for two reasons.
    - To give you a glimpse of a discovery I made that life is simple, but through our perceptions and emotions, we can make it complicated.
    - By focusing and implementing on one thing, you start the domino effect of change.
- I divided this book into sections to ease digestion and a summary of each section to understand at least the basis of *Life's One Law.*
- It is up to you to turn this potential knowledge, this dormant energy waiting to be expressed in your daily life.
- The big question for you to answer is: **Do I mark up this book with notes and insights or measure the amount of dust it can accumulate over time?**

SECTION 6: EXPLANATION OF TERMS

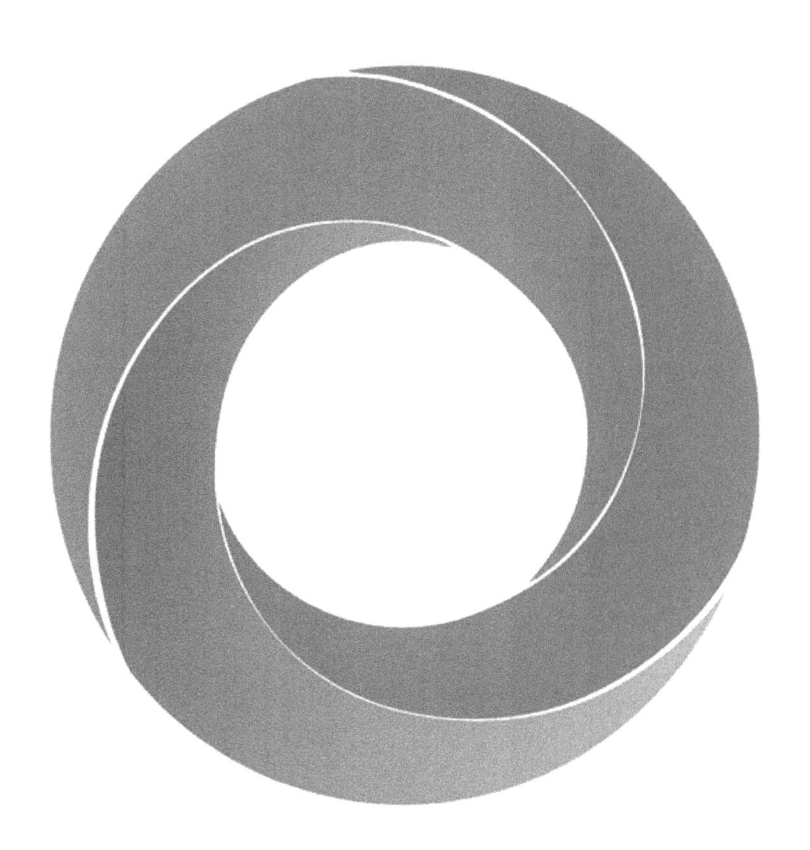

QUICK REFERENCE FOR *LIFE'S ONE LAW*

This reference can be used as a study guide to reinforce the teachings in this book. Many new ideas have been given to you and for you to easily and fully incorporate them into your business and daily life, I decided to summarize their meaning and use.

I suggest reviewing this section every day for 30 days and see what you could have done differently within your day to further your growth and profitability in all aspects of your life.

The Six Seasons: Each law is composed of two seasons with opposite functions. The seasons, as in life, can only move in one direction. Each season in your life can last from one second to years depending on how you fulfill its role in your business or in life. You can be in harvest in your personal life and autumn in your business. Each business deal or client can be in a separate season. By recognizing the season you are in relative to that relationship, you will determine what is needed to be done to fulfill its requirements. Once a season is fulfilled, it moves onto the next season causing you to understand what your next step will be.

Summer and Winter = The Director Principle
Harvest and Relinquis = The Supplier Principle
Autumn and Spring = The Communicator Principle

Summer: This is when your fruit (what you created in business and in life) is produced. From the knowledge and understanding of the quality and quantity of your fruit, you will determine how the other seasons performed and decide what to do from there. Do you merely monitor the seasons to continue your business and life as is or is it time for a change?

Harvest: It is time to gather, accept and replenish the knowledge obtained in summer and take for yourself. This season shows you it is time to give to yourself and be paid for your product or service in an even exchange.

Autumn: The season of detachment allows you to separate and remove what is no longer working in your business and life. This is where you create your Autumn List to detach from the people, things and events that are draining you of your vital resources.

Winter: The period of stillness, planning, and reflection within to envision your future summer. Here new ideas are created or old ones reorganized because of your unlimited potential. It is up to you how you sequence this potentiality and design it to show the world. Having the trust and faith in yourself and your higher power or your inner wisdom, gives you the power to emerge from this hibernation to continue your purpose in business and life.

Relinquis: Unfold your plan of winter and emerge to show the world your nectar, your product and service for them to feast upon to grow and prosper. How your burning desire and passion is sensed by the outside world will determine how attractive your product and service will be to your potential and/or current pollinators – your customers, employees, boss, friends, loved ones, etc.

Spring: This is when relationships are built. The effectiveness of your communication in this season will be determined by the rapport you have with them. Focusing on different pollinators and not just one or two will increase your chances of survival for a prosperous summer. This season gives you the opportunity to show your fruit and move into summer so that your customer can make a decision to hire you and pay for it in harvest.

True and Fear Seasons: Living in a dichotomous world where opposites reside, experiencing a season with either truth or fear may give you different consequences. A tree does not live in fear so it only experiences the effects of the True Seasons because it does not judge and accepts them as is. It will adapt to its environment to survive and continue to prosper until the next challenge or storm. Whether it lives to see another day or dies in that storm, its inner knowing that its remains will be used to continue to nourish something else and be consumed by it, just connects to a different purpose to be of service in another form. This whole process followed the True Seasons. Can you pick them out?

Words Summarizing the True Seasons

Summer (Decision)
Harvest (Replenish)
Autumn (Detach)
Winter (Plan)
Relinquis (Give)
Spring (Connect)

The Three R's – Roles, Rewards and Relationships.

Roles: These are the characters you play in life and how you deal with your life's direction and responsibilities.

Rewards: You can be rewarded with people, things or events that can give you a beneficial or detrimental consequence.

Relationships: The connection of any two or more entities. The strength of the rapport you have with them will be determined by the stability of the emotional bonds you have created.

Your Traits: These determine your behavior – your actions and reactions to every situation you encounter.

The Dominant Trait: Your "go-to" trait on which you rely, especially during times of stress.

The Mediator Trait: The bridge between the Dominant Trait and the Sabotaging Trait.

The Sabotaging Trait: This non-dominant trait brings your challenges and solutions in order to experience life to the fullest.

The Behavior Domino Effect: A chain reaction of different traits determined by the Personality Sequence.

The Sabotaging Trait and The Antidote: These determine whether the Behavior Domino Effect will cause you to protect yourself from your environment or use it for optimal growth.

The Personality Stress Sequence:

The arrangement of the three traits that are synonymous to the three principles.

The Director Trait: Taking control of your thoughts and staying on track.

The Supplier Trait: Desiring for an equal exchange so you feel good.

The Communicator Trait: Connecting to entities that will allow you to flourish.

The Principles and Your Traits:

The Three Principles rule every aspect of who you are. Your traits are the principles applied personally, since they govern or rule your behavior. Each principle governs each of your traits.

Director Principle = Director Trait = Thoughts
Supplier Principle = Supplier Trait = Feelings
Communicator Principle = Communicator Trait = Emotions

The Three Principles: The three principles explain individually how energy is directed, supplied, and communicated. They are:

The Director Principle
The Supplier Principle
The Communicator Principle

These principles cannot work independently from each other. Therefore, just as cells in your body make up the one entity called YOU, so too the principles make up *Life's One Law*. The cell and the body cannot exist without each other. *Life's One Law* also is intertwined and cannot exist without these three principles.

Life's One Law: This is Nature's Blueprint for Repeatable Success. Nature is synonymous with the universe as it uses the same design to create the smallest of the smallest to the largest of the largest. Energy exists because of it and it determines what happens to energy—where it goes, how it's used, and what it affects.

Life's One Law is you and everything that is around you. By reading this book, performing its exercises and making its teachings a part of you, then you can fully embrace and enjoy the fruits of your business and your life.

ADDITIONAL RECOMMENDATIONS

Dr. Philip Agrios is dedicated to guiding people and businesses into balance by understanding ***Life's One Law*** through Nature's Blueprint for Repeatable Success, uncovering their Sabotaging Trait and utilizing their Antidote for maximal health, wealth and happiness.

Visit our website at www.DrAgrios.com for:

Discover Your Sabotaging Trait and Antidote For Free: Take a quick quiz.

Mentoring Programs: Individualized one to one programs, designed to maximize your potential in business and in life through simple and powerful principles that work.

Speaking: Dr. Agrios shares how *Life's One Law* is the key to every successful person and business and its teams. Entertaining and engaging, people grasp how to change their outside circumstances, whether in business or in life, with the teachings of *Life's One Law*.

Workshops: Workshops allow owners, managers and employees to stop sabotaging themselves and perform at their maximum potential. They learn how to react differently to stressful situations by simply changing their behavior. They will discover how to enhance team building through better relationships within the company, with their customers and at home.

Courses & Products: Dr. Agrios has developed many courses and products so you can fully benefit from the teachings of *Life's One Law*.

Call Now at 732-383-5410 or visit the website www.DrAgrios.com

INDEX

A Return To Love................20
abundance.. 52, 187, 190, 203-207
acceptance 46, 63, 113
addictions......................19, 76, 81
anger.......................77, 94, 158
antidote......6, 159, 160, 172, 181-186, 195, 209, 210, 217, 219
anxiety.........72, 74, 157-159, 207
autoimmune disease...4, 35, 125, 201
autumn.......12, 29, 31, 35, 37-38, 42,47, 58, 64-67, 73-76, 78-80, 83-85, 92, 107, 115, 117-118, 123, 127-128, 131-132, 137-139, 152-153, 178-180, 193-194, 200, 203, 207, 214-216, 220, 221, 223
autumnize............74, 76, 78, 80
awareness........87, 124, 163-164
balance.......37, 43-44, 46, 48, 75, 113-115, 120-121, 123, 129-131, 147, 156-157, 159, 176, 185-186, 189, 190, 195, 199, 205, 219
behavior domino effect....158, 217
blueprint.......5-7, 20, 25-28, 30, 33-34, 40-41, 48, 64, 108, 119, 134, 147, 193, 195, 198, 209, 218-219
burning desire..........38-39, 61, 75, 95, 119, 121, 129, 178, 188, 199, 200, 203-206, 207, 209, 210, 215
challenges..........75, 112, 116, 140, 148, 156-157, 160, 177,181, 195, 217
change...... 4-8, 8, 13, 16-18, 28, 32, 34-36, 40-41, 44, 48-49, 53, 57, 59-61, 65, 70-71, 72, 74-75, 77, 79-80, 85, 91, 93-95, 101, 107-109, 115-118, 126-127, 132, 138-139, 142, 145, 152, 163, 175, 180, 183, 187, 190, 192-195, 200, 206, 208, 210, 211, 214
choices............70, 79, 94, 123, 163, 167, 191
chronic pain.........................18
color(s).......25, 26, 28, 91, 102, 161, 187
communication........40, 88, 93, 100, 102, 104-105, 144, 166, 169-170, 180, 183-184, 215
Communicator principle...154, 161-162, 166, 169, 171-172, 176-177, 180, 188, 199, 214, 218
Communicator Saboteur.....186
Communicator trait...162, 166, 169-170, 172, 217-218
connection.....32, 73-74, 77-78, 86, 91, 99-101, 121, 141, 166, 178, 216
consequences........6, 13, 34, 114, 120, 137, 141, 158, 194, 216
control.....4-8, 12, 14, 18, 34, 40, 55, 75, 92, 122, 126, 133, 136, 157-158, 163-164, 167-168, 176, 184, 185, 187

cycle of seasons..................34
desire..........8, 17, 36, 38-40, 46-47, 52, 59-61, 65-67, 75, 83-85, 90-96, 101, 107, 109, 113, 115, 118-121, 123, 126-130, 143, 158, 164, 168-169, 176-178, 188-190, 195, 198-200, 203-210, 215
detach, detaching...31, 64-66, 72-73, 77-84, 86-87, 117-118, 123, 128, 130-131, 170-171, 189, 195, 215
detachment...31, 65-66, 79-80, 87, 123, 138, 215
direction...8, 13, 40, 49, 54, 56, 67, 84-85, 148, 158, 161-162, 174-175, 179, 190, 199-200, 214, 216
Director principle...154, 161-162, 167, 171-172, 180, 183-184, 190, 192, 199, 214, 218
Director Saboteur.............184-185
Director trait.....162, 164, 167-168, 172, 174, 180, 217, 218
discernment.........188, 190, 192, 195, 210
disconnection....65-66, 74, 78, 166
diversify...............................101
dominant trait...155-157, 160, 167-170, 183-184, 209
Edison, Thomas A...................44
enzymes...............................152
exercises
  autumn list.......67, 73-80, 85-86, 92, 215
  gratitude list........................96
  harvest exercises...............62-63
  relationship exercise..........77-78
  relinquis exercise..............97-98
  rewards exercise...............73-74
  spring exercise..............103-105
  summer exercise...57-58, 109-110
  time management technique...68-69
  winter exercise.............87-88, 94
failure......5, 7, 16, 19, 35, 41, 42, 44-46, 48, 55, 61, 92, 108, 110, 119, 158-159
faith....119, 167, 175, 177, 185, 199, 209, 215
fear.....17, 20 47, 60-61, 71, 87, 95, 105, 112-126, 128-133, 135, 147, 149, 157, 182, 186, 190, 193-195, 200, 205, 216
Fear Seasons......124-125, 128-132, 198, 216
  Fear Autumn...............117, 130
  Fear Harvest................116, 130
  Fear Relinquis...................120
  Fear Spring.......................121
  Fear Summer...115, 122, 130, 207
  Fear Winter................118, 130
feelings.......6, 13, 34, 71-72, 78, 92, 105, 114, 120, 125-126, 137-138, 144, 161-162, 164-166, 168-170, 177, 180, 186, 201, 206, 210, 218
fighting.........................75, 199
forgive.......................92-94, 200
fruit....30, 32, 35-36, 37-40, 43, 53-54, 65, 73, 83, 85, 106, 108, 125, 127, 138, 176, 177, 190-191, 204,

214
gather.....30-31, 36-37, 58, 59, 61, 65-66, 107, 115, 141, 177, 210, 215
go-to trait....................................155
grateful, gratitude...46, 92, 93-96, 102, 123, 187, 200, 207, 221
growth season....................31-32
guidance............................118
harvest.........29-31, 33, 36-37, 41, 55, 58-66, 83-84, 107, 109, 115-116, 118, 127-130, 132, 136-137, 143, 146, 152-153, 176-177, 180, 188, 199, 203, 205-208, 214, 215
Higher Power...112, 118-119, 124, 192, 215
Hill, Napoleon........................90
imbalance.......46, 72, 75, 128, 130, 147, 155, 157, 159, 167, 175, 189, 206, 210
impatience...........39, 96, 107, 120, 187
invalidation.........................125
journal...............................83
Knight, Emily.........................25
lack.........46, 52-53, 65, 71, 79, 83-84, 109, 116, 130, 176, 184, 191
Lao-Tse..............................126
Law of Attraction...............39, 91
less dominant trait.................155
Life's One Law....7, 96, 148, 150, 154, 161-162, 164, 170-171, 173, 179-180, 189, 195, 208
loss..................12, 80, 118, 146
mediator......155, 157, 160, 167-169, 209, 217
meditation..................25, 118
money......10, 16-17, 19, 28, 42, 46-47, 59, 62, 69, 71-72, 75-76, 79, 84, 93, 97, 108-109, 114-115, 117, 129, 141, 144-147, 165, 204-205, 210
non-dominant trait....155, 167, 217
opportunity...46, 60-61, 74, 83, 93, 100, 125, 129, 147, 165, 215
overwhelm(ed)....10, 16, 26, 56, 72, 87, 102, 105, 113, 120-121, 171, 184-185, 210
pattern...........8, 34, 114, 171, 182
perception.....3-5, 8-9, 13, 18, 20, 43, 45, 47, 52, 54, 60, 65, 85, 114, 117, 123, 125, 132, 134-135, 145, 147, 163, 166-167, 187, 198, 211
personality stress sequence... 160-162, 167, 172, 183-184, 186, 209
perspective..........94, 112, 154, 161
Plato...............................158
Pollination.....................32, 93
pollinators...32, 39-40, 99, 100-102, 121, 142, 144, 215
potential....16-17, 19, 30-31, 35, 38-40, 47, 52-53, 70-71, 82-84, 90, 93-94, 96, 101,104, 108-109, 111, 116-121, 135, 137-138, 142, 144, 147, 175, 204, 207-208, 211, 215, 219
power....14, 16, 18, 20, 38-39, 82, 83, 90, 92, 94, 122, 127, 174-175,

177, 180, 187, 194-195, 211, 215
problem....19, 30, 44, 46-47, 54-57, 61, 65, 75, 84, 108, 112, 116, 135-136, 140-145, 148-149, 156-158, 169, 181, 187, 191, 200, 206
product......30, 32, 38, 53-54, 56, 58-59, 61, 70, 80, 91-92, 104, 107-110, 112-117, 119, 122-124, 131, 135-137, 141-147, 174-175, 177-178, 180, 183-184, 189, 199, 205, 215
production season..............30, 32
rapport..........99, 101-104, 121, 129, 131-132, 138, 215, 216
reality.......9-10, 30, 92, 126, 163-165
reflection...................84, 85, 215
relationships...7, 36, 43, 59, 63, 66, 72-78, 80-81, 94, 99-102, 105, 144, 193, 215, 216
relinquis......29, 31-32, 36, 38-39, 47, 52, 83, 90-93, 97, 100-103, 116, 119-121, 127, 129-130, 132, 142-144, 146, 153, 171, 176-177, 180, 188, 199, 203, 205, 207-208, 214
resistance.......60, 75, 138, 156, 181, 199-200, 204, 206, 210
rewards............62, 66, 69, 71, 73, 78, 94, 190, 216
road blocks..........................82
roles...............66, 68-69, 78, 81, 94, 97, 216
sabotage.................156, 184
sabotaging trait..........6, 155-159, 160, 167-170, 172, 180, 181-186, 187, 195, 209, 217, 219
.... Communicator Saboteur...186
..... Director Saboteur......184-185
.... Supplier Saboteur............185
seasons...7, 8, 25, 26, 28-29, 32-34, 34-35, 40-42, 45, 47-48, 53, 59-61, 65, 74-75, 88, 96, 107-108, 112, 114, 122-127, 128-133, 139, 145, 148-149, 152-153, 159, 161, 171, 173-174, 176-177, 187, 195, 198, 204, 210, 214, 216
selfishness....37, 43, 116, 120, 136-137, 175, 201
self-nourishment...................36
service..........30, 37, 53-54, 56, 58-59, 61-62, 68, 80, 92, 104, 107, 109, 111-117, 119, 121, 123-124, 131, 135-137, 141-147, 177-178, 183, 188-190, 193, 195, 199, 205, 207, 210, 215, 216
silent partner...139-143, 150-152, 165-170, 204
communicator...................169
director.........................168-169
supplier...............................169
solution.....16, 44, 46-47, 61, 85, 105, 126, 141-146, 159, 181-182, 204, 217
spring.......29, 31-32, 35, 39, 40, 42, 47, 52, 74, 91, 93, 99-107, 121, 123, 127, 129, 130-132, 144, 152, 178, 180, 193-194, 200, 203, 206-

207, 214-216
stillness……………..……38, 82, 215
storage season……………….…..31
stress….4, 6, 34-36, 43, 66, 70, 72, 95, 103, 105, 112, 114, 117-118, 125, 134, 138, 144, 149, 155-157, 160-162, 167, 170, 172, 184, 186, 209, 217, 219
summer…...29-30, 32-33, 35-36, 38-40, 52-56, 59, 64-65, 82-83, 85, 87, 99, 100, 102, 106-111, 115, 118, 122, 124-125, 127-130, 132, 134-135, 137-138, 140-142, 145-146, 149, 153, 171-177, 180, 190, 191, 192, 199, 203-204, 207, 210, 214-216
supplier principle…..154, 161-164, 168, 171-172, 176-177, 180, 188, 199, 214, 218
Supplier Saboteur………………185
supplier trait……………162, 164-165, 168-169, 172, 180, 217, 218
supply..17, 31, 36, 65, 91, 101, 139, 158, 164-165, 169-170, 177, 180, 200-201, 204
surrender, surrendering….32, 38-40, 91-92, 119
synonymity………………………46
Taoism…………………….....126
The Fairy That Wanted More…...15
timeline……………………....35
time management technique…68-69
traits….6, 9, 75, 154-155, 160-172, 174, 180-186, 187, 195, 209, 217
true seasons….122-123, 125, 128, 132, 198, 204, 216
True Autumn………………117
True Harvest……………115-116
True Relinquis………......119-121
True Spring……………….121
True Summer……...115, 122, 207
True Winter…………….118, 207
trust……....34, 47, 61, 79-80, 95, 114, 118-119, 122-124, 127, 131-132, 145, 167, 175, 182, 185, 189, 199, 209, 215
underproduction…..……...48, 60
unsuccessful………...16, 18, 198
vibration…45, 126, 144, 206, 208
weight loss…………………..16
wholeness season…………….32
Williamson, Marianne……….20
winter…29, 31-32, 37, 40, 47, 52, 59, 64, 82-87, 90-91, 94, 100, 107-108, 113, 118-119, 121, 127, 128-130, 132, 138-139, 141-143, 145-146, 152-153, 173-177, 180, 190-192, 199, 201, 203-204, 207, 209, 214
workaholic……………….43, 76